Psalms of Joy and Faith

By the same author

PREACHING FROM THE PROPHETS
ESSENTIALS OF BIBLICAL HEBREW

PSALMS OF JOY AND FAITH

Kyle M. Yates

Broadman Press
Nashville, Tennessee

Dewey Decimal Classification: 223.2

Printed in the United States of America

DEDICATED
to
MY WIFE

a devoted lover
a treasured helper
a constant inspiration
a consecrated Christian

CONTENTS

PREFACE

YOU HAVE A TREASURE. YOU HAVE HEARD OF "ACRES OF diamonds." How about the rich gems that are at your very finger tips? For three thousand years men have been in possession of these priceless poems. Holy men of God prepared them for perplexed hearts. They hold the remedy so sorely needed in our generation. When hungry hearts find the living truths new strength is given for daily living. A vital faith in the eternal God springs up within the soul. Clearly and distinctly a new pattern takes shape. Hope is born afresh in the inner being. Pain and sorrow and grief lose their terrors. Fear flies away as the sacred pages reveal hidden truths uttered by men of the long ago who won victories in the same arenas. Life takes on new meaning as the plan of God is viewed in its full perspective. Instead of doubt and impatience and despair one finds himself rejoicing in the safety of God's marvelous presence. In some strange way the heart is stilled as if by a magic wand when the troubled child feels the cooling touch of the divine fingers.

God is in the Psalms. He reveals Himself as a precious Companion, always alert, available, interested, able, anxious to provide every gift that His beloved children can need. Every tragic situation is met by One who knows how to deal with the delicate strands of the heart with tenderness and care. In each spot a frail human being with very little equipment for meeting trials and sufferings found a strange and precious guidance by turning to God. Every phase of life is pictured. Joys, victories, struggles, defeats, shameful disgraces, and monotonous plodding come in for their place in human experience. Any experience in a man's life can find its picture in these ageless poems. The solution for all of life's problems can be discovered in these pages. Human interest stories call the reader on from page to page.

Why not preach these challenging messages? Why not take thirty minutes in the home to read one of these psalms and interpret its truths in terms that will grip the attention of young and old alike? Our people will be interested. They will follow you with rapt attention. They will be eager for the next study. The preaching of expository sermons will be easy. The truths will be presented in an orderly manner and will be interpreted so as to apply to the hearts and minds of all age groups. The mind of the minister or the teacher will be enriched. The members of the congregation or class will be blessed more richly than you can imagine.

In the presentation of these studies the author has been mindful of questions of authorship, text, integrity and various readings. In each case full consideration has been given to the matters involved. The interpretation given is in the light of the author's decisions in each case. It does not seem advisable to record the critical structure as the work proceeds. Students will find it easy to consult technical commentaries and grammars for the complete story.

In the main I have attempted to use the King James Version as a basis for the scripture quotations. In many instances, however, I have taken the liberty of changing the word so as to bring out more clearly the exact meaning. The finished text as found in this volume is perhaps most definitely influenced by the special edition put out by the Judson Press in 1913 known as *The Holy Bible, an Improved Edition*. It is a joy to acknowledge my debt to this translation. I have also been definitely influenced by all of my colleagues on the committee for the *Revised Standard Version*.

No one is more mindful of the debt due other contributors. So many commentaries and books have been read and digested

that it would be impossible to give full credit for transla-
tions, ideas, interpretations, homiletical thoughts, and practical applications. Let it be clearly understood that gratitude
is expressed for all the help that has come. My prayer is that
many, many hearts may be richly blessed as these pages sug-
gest rich truths for needy souls.

I am indebted to each member of my family and members
of the great Second Baptist Church of Houston for valuable
suggestions, sympathetic encouragement, and wise counsel.
My son, Rev. Kyle M. Yates, Jr., has proved particularly
valuable to me in the preparation of the manuscript. My heart
goes out in grateful acknowledgment. Rich joys will be mine
as I find these studies used and enjoyed by those who love
the Psalms.

KYLE M. YATES

Houston, Texas
March 1, 1948

PREACHING FROM THE PSALMS

I

OUT OF THE DEPTHS

PSALM 51

Have mercy upon me, O God, according to thy loving-kindness, according to the multitude of thy tender mercies blot out my transgressions. Wash me thoroughly from my iniquity, and cleanse me from my sin. For I acknowledge my transgressions, and my sin is ever before me. Against thee, thee only, have I sinned, and done this evil in thy sight. . . . Purge me with hyssop, and I shall be clean; wash me, and I shall be whiter than snow. Make me to hear joy and gladness, that the bones which thou hast broken may rejoice. Hide thy face from my sins, and blot out all my iniquities. Create in me a clean heart, O God, and renew a right spirit within me. Cast me not away from thy presence, and take not thy Holy Spirit from me. Restore to me the joy of thy salvation, and uphold me with thy free Spirit. Then will I teach transgressors thy ways, and sinners shall be converted unto thee. Deliver me from bloodguiltiness, O God, thou God of my salvation, and my tongue shall sing aloud of thy righteousness. . . . The sacrifices of God are a broken spirit; a broken and contrite heart, O God, thou wilt not despise.

How can a preacher be so heartless as to pull aside a curtain and invite his listeners to look upon a spectacle so private, so personal, so indicative of soul agony as a consideration of Psalm 51 makes necessary? One finds himself on the verge of an apology as he attempts such a cruel step. For almost three thousand years men have come to this sacred spot and have been strangely moved by the tragic picture they have gazed upon. The lure of it has not been a mere curious look upon the pathetic struggle of a hero who fought and wrestled and writhed in soul agony without a sublime victory. The spectators have looked on in breathless wonder as they have witnessed the helpless man deal with a problem that clearly has no human solution. They have listened while sobs and confessions shake the body and hot tears burn his face and fears of eternal banishment from God's presence chill the very marrow in his bones. They are amazed as the full significance of the sufferer's plight sweeps over them. He is guilty of sins that forever put him beyond the remedy provided in the law. Though a king of an oriental kingdom with soldiers and mighty men to do his bidding he is now seen as a helpless sinner, naked and defenseless, without any possible means of escape or deliverance. With multitudes of bulls and rams and goats at his disposal he finds that all of these put together will not cleanse him or make him fit for his Maker's presence. While we watch with bated breath, this lone man goes doggedly about the supreme business of getting his soul washed and cleansed and restored and created anew. The joybells ring again as the glow of a new presence gives them utterance. Before our very eyes he becomes a new creature, singing a new song, witnessing to his sinner friends of the manifold mercy of God, and bringing many new converts to Him who gave him the victory. Let us look on reverently and thoughtfully as we catch his secret and understand the true way to cleansing and restoration and power.

DAVID, BATHSHEBA, URIAH, NATHAN

To begin at the right place we must look upon a court scene in Jerusalem with Israel's greatest king sitting on the throne. He had been divinely chosen and anointed and endowed and sustained for the task of being God's king on His choice throne. He had become the nation's spiritual leader and had set up the worship of Jehovah in the land. Clean and sensitive and capable of the highest spiritual triumphs, he had been promised that his house should be established forever. Already many psalms had come from his hand. The kingdom had been built up, enemies were beaten before his armies, and neighboring princes hastened to bend the knee to him.

In the midst of all this victory and luxury, David saw and wanted and took for himself the beautiful wife of Uriah, the Hittite. Any other king could have done this without a whisper of blame upon him, but David was Jehovah's anointed and must not sin. Before the story was finished, murder was added to the ugly picture when Uriah was executed to make the black deed complete. Thus adultery and murder clung to his blackened soul.

For almost a year David endured the lashing of an active conscience and sought to make himself and those about him believe that all was well. One day the fearless Nathan came with the powerful thrust that left the king conscious of his sin and able to sense something of his tragic condition before a just and holy God. His heart was crushed before the sharp *thou art the man*. He readily admitted: *I have sinned against Jehovah*. No effort at self-improvement could help. He did not call a priest or present burnt offerings. He knew too well how useless such remedies would be in his desperate plight. His broken and contrite heart groaned for deliverance. Only God could help him. It was the most tragic moment of his life. The tempter had won his victory. The one person in the entire world most desired by the evil kingdom had been trapped and bound and ruined. It must have called forth a big celebration in the devil's realm. David, the spiritual leader of God's chosen people, was out of the fight. What a pity!

A CRY FOR FORGIVENESS (1, 2)

Man's greatest need is for forgiveness. David saw God as one to whom he must answer, as one from whom he must obtain mercy, and as one whom he could trust for mercy and pardon. He was just as certain that no human power or resource could avail in his tragic plight. Before he mentions his sin, he appeals to God for mercy. He does not, at that moment, dare say: "My God," for that would have been presumption. His sin had alienated him from God. He could stand a long way off and cry: *Have mercy upon me, O God.* It is the cry of a guilty soul who dreads justice and who longs for mercy. Such sins as his could not be touched except by the hand of a merciful God. Confidently he turns to God for the pardon, the forgiveness, the cleansing, and the restoration that his heart craves.

His first move is to spread out his particular acts of sin against his God. He uses three words to picture the different aspects of sin. *Pesha* means "rebellion," "transgression"— setting one's self against the will and law of God. It is an act of high treason against the Sovereign of the universe. *Awon,* "iniquity," means that which is "twisted" or "warped" or "crooked." It is in reality depravity of conduct. *Hattath,* "sin," means literally "missing in the aim or the mark." Sin is error, failure, a blunder. Man misses God's high destiny for his life. These sins were before him as prominent hills dominating the landscape. As he looked upon these hills he realized that deep underneath them lay the pool out of which sins grew. In that inner depth he recognized a vitiated nature that no earthly remedy could change. He was far more concerned about sin than sins. His sin was his great worry. In desperation he fell back upon the eternal promises of covenant love. He was confident that he could trust a loving God to work a miracle. He would cast himself on the mercy of One who had the power and the love to work it out.

The three verbs he uses would indicate that the sinner wants God to do something for him that he cannot do for himself. He says: *Blot out, wash me, cleanse me*. Blot out the record of the rebellion against God. Only He has that record and He alone can erase it from the book. In addition to the work on the record, he wants something done to his own vile body and mind and soul. He says: *Wash me thoroughly*. His whole being is defiled and the dye is deeply ingrained. It will take rough work, repeated scrubbings, painful removal to effect the kind of cleansing that his soul longs for now that he has realized how foul and sinful he is.

It is not enough to *blot out* and *wash*. He wants to be absolutely clean inside and out so that the holy eyes of God can be pleased with what they see when they examine him. David is literally sick of sin and wants it all removed by water or by fire or by any other drastic method so that every vestige of the vile stuff may be eliminated. David is not concerned about the punishment or the consequences of sin. He is set on getting rid of sin itself. He knows something of the defiling nature of sin and how foul one is as he stands under the divine eye. He has no hesitation in claiming all the sin and its defilement as his very own. Sin is his own personal property. He knows that no one else can lay claim to it. He assumes full responsibility for every particle of the total mass of sin that he carries. He is urging God to remove it all and leave him as clean and sweet and innocent as a newborn baby.

In his eyes sin is a burden to be removed, a pollution to be washed out, a bondage that must be taken away, a polluted robe that must be made clean, a blotted record that must be expunged, a fatal disease that must be cured. God alone can work these miracles. In humble spirit he prays for God to work the miracle.

A Sincere Confession (3-6)

God does not need to accuse this penitent sinner. He says: *I acknowledge my transgressions, and my sin is ever before me*. Nathan had said: "Thou art the man." David is now saying: "I am the man." His repentance has led him far enough along the road to deliverance that he openly confesses his own sin. A great and good man such as the saintly David must have been covered with shame to confess publicly such vile sins, but he comes willingly forward with the full and open confession. He frankly assumes full responsibility for the sins. No ancestor is blamed for hereditary tendencies or weaknesses. Bathsheba, though indiscreet and willing to be led astray, is not saddled with even a small part of the blame. The current social standards are not listed among the extenuating circumstances. The fact that he had no one else among his associates to help carry the high standard is not mentioned to ease the blow. He openly declares to God that he, and he alone, is wholly responsible for the sins of which he is so ashamed. His own conscience is now his constant accuser. He admits that he is a sinful man, born of a sinful woman, held down by sin's power. He wants to be free from sin. Even thoughtful people today must go a long way to reach the high point to which David came in this clear understanding of the place and power of full confession of sin.

Prayer for Full Cleansing (7-9)

The psalmist prays not only to be received into God's presence again, but that he may be fit for His presence. With an unusual burst of fervor the psalmist comes back with his earnest plea for cleansing and for restoration. It is always a vital matter to one who has seen the holy God and who has seen the full view of his own vile, sinful self. His is a genuine prayer for the touch that will cleanse and purify and sweeten the whole sin-defiled being. When God has completed the painful operation, he wants God to sprinkle the hyssop upon him indicating the full divine approval. He wants the sanctifying process as well as the pardoning process to be operative in him.

When he is pardoned and then made clean, he begs that joy and gladness may be his portion again. It is pathetic to hear the mighty David begging God to bring back the old joy to his saddened heart. Sin had taken the music out of his life. He longs for the ringing of the bells in his soul once more. It will be a new day for him when he can *hear* the heavenly music in his own soul again. Has it occurred to you that such a prayer would be preposterous anywhere except at the throne of God? He alone can restore the music to the soul. Again David begs God to turn His eyes away from the sins that are constantly in his memory. It will be good to know that God is not looking upon them.

Prayer for a New Heart and a New Life (10-12)

Is it not too bad that when sin has had its way in a heart that God must be called in to act as Creator again? What destructive power sin must have! David has prayed for cleansing and restoration and reclaiming. He now boldly asks God for a new heart. Repairs are out of the question. A new heart is necessary. The old nature is helpless. The Creator must do His work all over again. The process must be a divine one. The whole man has been infected with poison. The whole man must share in the remedy. The spiritual leper must be cleansed in mind, in will, in conscience. David is laying here the foundation for the New Testament doctrine of the New Birth and the New Life. He recognizes the strategic importance of being born again. The heart must be a new one. His whole mental, moral, and spiritual self must be renewed by the creative touch of God. It is a fervent prayer for holiness. The new creature must be freed, must be sanctified, must be renewed. He must be able to stand in God's presence, without shame, and with joy and radiance lighting his voice and his countenance. "The expulsive power of a higher affection" must bring about a mysterious change in his whole being.

Pathetically the psalmist begs God to keep him close and not banish him from His presence. Cain was banished to wander alone outside the range of God's loving care. Others who became utterly unclean had been cast away. David pleads with God that he be allowed to stay near the One who forgives and cleanses and restores. He cannot live away from the divine light even though he recognizes that he deserves such treatment as was accorded the leper. He cannot bear to think of having to live without the presence of the Holy Spirit to guide and direct his steps, to interpret the meaning of God's will, to encourage and strengthen him in all his work, and to give him the strength and assurance for every duty and for every assignment. Since that day in Bethlehem when the old prophet anointed him, he has enjoyed the strange exhilaration of God's continuing presence. He prays that this Spirit may not be taken away from him as was true in the case of Saul.

Then like a hungry boy he prays: *Give me back the joys which once were mine.* What a loss he had sustained! How empty life is when there is no music! How true it is that sin keeps us from joy! It is a great prayer that he utters when he asks that full happiness be restored to him. Many church members who once found indescribable joy in the worship and service of the Lord are now living empty lives. How appropriate this prayer for their lives! May God help us all to utter such a prayer from the heart.

A GRAND ASSURANCE (7-12)

Throughout each of these earnest petitions we have seen an assurance that God will hear and answer. The entire psalm is grounded in the knowledge that the psalmist's prayers are to be answered. No doubt is manifested in any of the verses. He knows God well enough to be certain of pardon and forgiveness and cleansing and restoration. He knows the possibilities of grace. He is certain there is a way out for the sinner. Hear him as he says: *Purge me . . . I shall be clean. Wash me and I shall be whiter than snow.* How could such a guilty sinner expect a holy God to make him clean? How could anyone hope to be whiter than snow? All the dyers on earth cannot dye a red into a white. How can a sinner whose sins are deeper than scarlet have such faith? The psalmist knew God better than many of us. He knew that no work was beyond His infinite power. He dared give utterance to a faith in the cleansing touch that would make the vilest sinner clean.

When this hope dawns, a man's life begins. Faith like this gives to you life's basic requirements. You find a truth to live by and a truth to die by. There is much of this assurance in the Bible. When Isaiah said: *Though your sins be as scarlet, they shall be as white as snow; though they be red like crimson, they shall be as wool,* he was only stating what had become his through his study of David's immortal lines and through his own experience with a forgiving God. Thank God for a faith that dared lay hold on the promises of God and plead for a cleansing that would go beyond the fondest dream of the majority of our people today. How marvelous it would be if we could visualize the full cleansing that God has in store for all men! Now that we have Christ's completed work on Calvary that has provided the "fountain filled with blood, drawn from Immanuel's veins," why cannot men look in faith to Him who is able to make us whiter than snow? Do you know one who needs to be washed in the blood of the Lamb? Will you help him see himself as God sees him and then lead him to pour out his confession to God as he prays to be washed until he is whiter than snow? He need have no question about it. Our Saviour will save unto the uttermost anyone who comes to Him.

A SACRED VOW (13-17)

The first impulse of a saved individual is to tell to others the merits of the glorious remedy that has saved him. David promises to seek out his friends who have fallen in the same pit and who need the same cleansing to tell them the good news. He knows the full depths to which they have plunged and the deep hunger of soul that plagues them. He understands the one and only method by which they can find forgiveness and cleansing. He knows the certainty of God's redeeming grace. He has just experienced the joy that comes when one is redeemed and restored. His witness will be most effective because men can see what has taken place in him. He vows that the rest of his life will be spent in telling of God's grace and in urging sinners to come to the one and only source of life and cleansing. He will be an evangelist, a seeker of lost men, an announcer of good news to those who languish in darkness and sin. His gospel will be a New Testament gospel. God's love for all men will be his theme. He is just as certain of victory here as he has been in his other prayers. He says: *and sinners shall be converted to thee.* What confidence that man has in God's saving power and in the effectiveness of a redeemed sinner's witness! It is amazing to follow him in the reaches of his faith. He who had, by his own example, taught others to sin now seeks to lead them back to God, assuring them that they will find in the wealth of His covenant love the pledge of all human blessedness. Others might despise these sinners, but he will dedicate his life to the task of winning them to his God.

Again he promises: *My tongue shall sing aloud of thy righteousness and my mouth shall show forth thy praise.* He will do personal witnessing and he will sing aloud praise to his God. Both preaching and singing will find a place in his future activities. Anything that will cause men to turn their thoughts to God and to surrender their hearts to Him will be in the realm of his work as a redeemed child of God. The psalmist resolves to use his regained freedom in grateful service and to express his thanksgiving by that sacrifice which is most pleasing to God.

In the midst of his vows he stops to restate his conception of the way to please God. He recognizes that he has a great mass of guilt written against him on the books of God. Once more he prays that he might be delivered from that guilt. His mind turns to the sanctuary and to the priestly offerings that were being burned to appease God for sins of omission and commission. Instantly he realizes how inadequate and useless they are for sins like his. He would be only too glad to furnish thousands of burnt offerings but he knows that they cannot effect the salvation he needs. He then gives expression to that classic statement: *The sacrifices of God are a broken spirit; a broken and a contrite heart, O God, thou wilt not despise.* Genuine repentance is the truest sacrifice that can be offered. David not only understood the clear requirement of God but he demonstrated in the most complete manner the exact will of God in that experience. In verses sixteen and seventeen, he is but writing out in brief form exactly what he has already put into actual practice. Crimes like David's could not be purged by any animal sacrifice. There was a death penalty prescribed for each of the two crimes. He deserved to die and he knew it. He cast himself on the mercy of God and pleaded with Him, saying, *Deliver me from bloodguiltiness.* He laid on the altar his own sinful heart and begged God to cleanse and re-create and restore his whole being so that he might be a useful instrument again. It is almost too perfect. It worked. David was a new creature under the cleansing fire of God, who heard his cry and answered his humble prayer.

Lest someone get the idea that verse seventeen holds up the vanquished and defeated and overwhelmed as the ideal members of Christ's redeemed group let us hasten to say that while humility and repentance and faith are the only gates to salvation, those who render an acceptable sacrifice to God are the victors and not the vanquished. They have struggled with evil and the evil one and have conquered them. They are, in Christ Jesus, stouthearted conquerors who move on from victory to victory because of the new life through Him. They can do all things through Christ who strengthens them.

CONCLUSION

Someone has said that certain notes dominate the music of this psalm. First, the note of SIN comes in (1, 2). It is regarded as a blotted record that must be expunged, a polluted robe which needs to be washed, a fatal disease which must be cleansed. It is *transgression, iniquity, sin.* The only remedy comes after one has acknowledged it. The second note is that of PERSONAL RESPONSIBILITY. The ever-recurring personal pronoun indicates David's willingness to assume full responsibility for his sorry plight. The third note is that of REPENTANCE. It was genuine sorrow for sin itself that produced heartfelt repentance and open confession. He was ready to turn his back on sin forever. The fourth note relates to FORGIVENESS (7-14). He knows God well enough to know that He will purge him, wash him, renew him, gladden him, deliver him, and restore him by means of creating in him a clean heart. The last note is that of TESTIMONY (12, 13, 15). It is the duty, the privilege and the joy of the rescued saint to go out and find others who are lost and bring them to light and life and salvation. Personal testimony will guarantee many new souls for the Master.

What a glorious psalm it is for the preacher, the teacher, the Christian, and for the lost sinner. It reveals the power and grip of sin, the love and mercy of God, the certain way of salvation, the assurance of healing, cleansing, divine forgiveness, and the sincere response of one who has been redeemed and restored. May God speak a powerful message to each heart through these ageless words.

II
THE JOY OF FORGIVENESS

PSALM 32

Blessed is he whose transgression is forgiven, whose sin is covered. Blessed is the man to whom the Lord imputes not iniquity, and in whose spirit there is no guile. When I kept silence, my bones wasted away through my groaning all the day long. For day and night thy hand was heavy on me. I acknowledged my sin unto thee, and my iniquity have I not hid. I said, I will confess my transgressions to the Lord; and thou forgavest the iniquity of my sin. . . . I will instruct thee and teach thee in the way which thou shalt go; I will guide thee with my eye.

WHO is the happiest person you know? Is he so radiantly happy that he must go about telling everyone what has happened to him? David has had something come into his life that has awakened the joybells and they are ringing with reckless abandon. In Psalm 51 he promised the Lord that he would spend the rest of his life telling others of his salvation so that sinners might be converted and turned to God. This psalm gives us the account of that effort. He is now doing his best to tell what happened to him and how any other person may have the same joys for himself. His heart leaps within him for he is now at peace with God and his sins have been washed away. He has been pardoned, cleansed, forgiven, restored, and given a new heart. Every prayer that he prayed has been answered literally and instantly. He begged God for all these blessings and then made some vows that he would be a flaming witness among the very friends who had been led astray by his own sinful life. He now has that supreme happiness which God alone can give. He is living because God has re-created him for the highest living. His desire is to tell all the world what God can do for a sinner who turns to Him in genuine repentance. Read carefully Psalm 51 and then turn to Psalm 32 to watch the picture unfold. It will be a revelation to you.

INTRODUCTION (1, 2)

Immediately we are confronted with a ringing declaration that not only gives an accurate picture of the experience of a human soul but rewards us with a universal truth that will transform lives. Each of us needs to listen to the man. Words fail him as he tries to tell how happy a man can be when his sins are rolled away and the conscience is stilled. He has found an inner peace that is indescribable. Forgiveness has brought joy and blessedness. He makes it perfectly clear that penitence is the indispensable condition for receiving this rich blessing.

Just as in Psalm 51 David refers to sin under three titles: *Pesha* is rebellion against God's authority or doing that which is expressly forbidden; *Hattath* is sin or missing the mark; and *Awon* is iniquity or moral distortion or crookedness. These three aspects of sin were present in the heart of David. He recognized each of them. He knew the power that sin exerted in a heart. Each of these aspects of sin had been manifest in his own life. He knew that human efforts to deal with sin could avail nothing. God must deal with sin.

After his prayer of heartfelt repentance God did something about it. He gives us three words to describe God's part in the process. Forgiveness is spoken of under three titles: the *transgression* must be *lifted up*, taken away, borne away by a vicarious sacrifice; the *sin* must be *covered*, hidden from the sight of God; *iniquity* must not be reckoned to his account, *canceled*. The union of the three words for sin makes up the full picture of sin in the heart. The union of these three Hebrew verbs is full remission or forgiveness.

The sinner who had been so completely contaminated by sin now finds himself free from the hated thing because God has seen to it that it is borne away on the innocent person of a sinless Substitute. God's eyes no longer have to look upon the vile spectacle. The record book is clean, too, for the iniquity is not recorded against him. It has been canceled. Is there any wonder that the sinner is radiantly happy? His sins are completely forgiven. They are gone from him forever. The dark writing has been canceled. He is at peace with God.

The New Testament gospel is a commentary on this psalm. God bears away, covers, cancels the record of my rebellion, my errors, my crookedness. The Lamb of God came to take my sin and bear it away. He died in order that the debt might be paid, that my sins might be laid on Him and taken away, covered and forever canceled. If your sins are not taken away by this Lamb of God they will remain and crush you. If God does not cover your sins they will lie there in plain view of the holy eyes of God and cry out for your punishment. If that black page of your sinful record is not wiped clean by His own blood then the forbidding record will stand there forever. Yes, my dear friend, *the blood of Jesus Christ cleanses us from all sin*. David had the story exactly right. No wonder he was happy. The condition laid down is that there must be absolute sincerity. No guile or deceit is in the heart. The repentance is real. He has not sought to deceive himself nor to deceive God. Openly, frankly, honestly he has poured out his fullest confession. No extenuating circumstance has been offered as an excuse. The holy heart of God has been fully satisfied with David's part and He has found delight in taking the sin away. In God's sight he is clean. Incredible joy now floods his soul.

A Dark Memory (3, 4)

The author, pausing to look back on that horrible nightmare, tells how sin served him and how severely he suffered while sin ruled over him. We may well listen for he is not spinning a thin theory for us. He is giving the straight picture of what happened in his own experience. He chose to cover his own sin and keep silent about it. He refused to acknowledge it to himself or to God. Why should he admit his sin? He found out how tragic it is to refuse to confess sin. His bones ached and rotted away causing excruciating agony. The hand of God was heavy upon him, and all through the night pain sapped his vitality so completely that he was increasingly miserable. He knew the misery of sullen silence. He could thank God that his conscience was still alive and that the hand of God was still heavy upon him. That man is to be pitied who does not feel the hand of God upon him. David was acutely aware of his sin and the strong efforts of God to bring him to his knees in sincere repentance. In spite of this he obstinately refused to surrender. How stubborn man is! To what lengths he will go to thwart God in His desires to forgive and cleanse and restore! David could not forget the miserable hours he spent in stubborn silence.

Confession and Forgiveness (5)

Finally David came to himself and saw clearly the way of restoration, the pathway to light and forgiveness. He said: *I began to make known to thee my sin, and mine iniquity I did not hide.* He confessed his sin as *sin*, as *transgression*, and as *iniquity*—the very same words he had used earlier to reveal the three aspects of sin. He did not attempt to conceal anything. It was all open before his God. He chose the way to full forgiveness. It is the only way. No other road to the light, to happiness, to life, is to be found anywhere. It is God's way to victory and peace and forgiveness. Why does a man continue to cover his own sin and suffer untold miseries when he could find deliverance and joy and peace and salvation by full confession and childlike trust in our Sin-bearer who bore in His own body our sins on the tree? David's words here constitute a warning against stubborn silence and an encouragement to come to Him who forgives and redeems and saves. If one so foul and unclean and low as the sinful David could find mercy and forgiveness surely any man anywhere can come with boldness to our Saviour. *For we have not a high priest which cannot be touched with the feeling of our infirmities; but was in all points tempted like as we are, yet without sin. Let us therefore come boldly unto the throne of grace, that we may obtain mercy, and find grace to help in time of need.*

With something that closely resembles a shout David says: *Thou forgavest the iniquity of my sin.* How that statement stirs our hearts, even today! He felt his burden fall off immediately. God had heard his humble cry for forgiveness and, without a moment's delay, had granted full pardon. He is always swifter to forgive than we are to confess. In this graphic story of David's experience we have seen sin committed, sin concealed, sin confessed, and sin covered, forgiven, canceled. What a glorious climax to that story! David was not only free from the worry and misery of sin but he was cleansed and purified from sin's foul touch. He was restored to full life again with a clean body and mind and a newly created heart ready to live the abundant life. The bells have been set going again and—best of all—he has been fully forgiven. No dark, blotched record remains against him. The pardoning grace of God has provided a means whereby the sinner's sins are borne far away and covered from God's sight and the ugly record has been washed completely away. In our own relationship with our Saviour we can witness the very same victory over sin and its foul touch. We have One who bore our sins away and willingly died on the cross that His blood might wash us clean. We are forgiven and cleansed and made new creatures when we confess our sins and trust Him for salvation.

A GRATEFUL TESTIMONY (6, 7)

In keeping with the purpose of the psalm we now find David bringing an exhortation to all others who might listen. He wants every soul to be certain of the joys that come to one who is pardoned, and he speaks of the folly of hardening the heart against a God who is so graciously ready to receive all who turn to Him in penitence. How can one fail to realize the glories of the pathway to light and life and peace of mind?

David knows so well what he endured, how he suffered, what he missed, how he found peace and joy, and how happy it made God's heart. He wants everyone to know something of the new faith he has in God. He knows that God can be found, that He will hear the prayer of an earnest seeker, that He has mercy and pardon in abundance, that He provides security and makes the soul safe in the *great waters*, and that He provides a safe stronghold where His redeemed ones may live in safety and in plenty. In the New Testament gospel this idea is made even richer and fuller. The Christian who has had his sins taken away *is hid with Christ in God*. Abundant songs of praise will be a part of his everyday experience because *he is kept by the power of God*. Secure in his strong mountain island he can watch the swirling floods as they beat helplessly against the rock on which he clings for he knows that he is eternally safe from storm and flood and satanic hand. He tells us that it is only through forgiveness that we come into that close communion with God that ensures absolute security in all disasters.

Rock of Ages, cleft for me,
Let me hide myself in Thee;
Let the water and the blood,
From Thy wounded side which flowed,
Be of sin the double cure,
Save from wrath and make me pure.

Nothing in my hand I bring,
Simply to Thy cross I cling;
Naked, come to Thee for dress;
Helpless, look to Thee for grace;
Vile, I to the fountain fly,
Wash me, Saviour, or I die.

Faith in God gives the sweetest assurance of the gripping power of the unseen hand. It is worth all the millions that can be found. How can an unsaved man continue to make his way through all the disasters and loneliness and fears that surround him on every hand? How can he ignore the certainty of an eternal hell that awaits everyone who does not have the Lord Jesus Christ as his advocate in that hour of judgment? How can he refuse to open the door and let the loving Saviour in when the peace that passes all understanding is available for him by faith in that Saviour? Life on this earth is nothing without Him. Life on the other shore is unspeakably horrible unless He is your Saviour. Why not open your heart to Him now? Why not let Him work His healing, forgiving work in you?

THE LORD SPEAKS TO THE PSALMIST (8, 9)

Two brief verses tell us God's word for our hearts. He is the Teacher, the Guide, the Leader of His own redeemed ones. He promises special guidance (8) and warns against obstinacy (9). He wants to teach them how to walk in the way. He says: *I will instruct thee, I will teach thee, I will guide thee.* Literally the first verb is, *I will make you to understand.* It is the divine way to make clear the way, point out the dangers and snares, lead to the refreshing waters, direct the work and the activities, light up the ravines and defiles with His own light, and show the many opportunities for helpful ministries along the road. Then He says: *I will counsel thee. My eyes shall be upon thee.* What a blessing is ours with the way made plain by the divine Guide! He will not leave us to our own inadequate understanding but will provide the daily guidance that will make our pilgrimage happy and safe and triumphant.

How tragic to find men who have surrendered their divinely given ability as a human being and have no more understanding than a beast! Brute animals must be controlled and curbed and compelled by force to submit to man's will. Bits and bridles and whips and spurs are used to force brutes to do as man demands. Men who refuse to come to God in penitence and obey His wishes, naturally lower themselves to the level of brute beasts and must expect severe discipline.

CONCLUSION (10, 11)

The psalmist hastens to contrast the lot of the righteous with that of the wicked. Calamities and chastisements will be the lot of those who choose to continue in their sins while the loving God will surround the trustful ones with mercies.

In the light of the tremendous contrast how can a forgiven soul refrain from shouting and praising God? Gratitude and rejoicing will be poured out in a literal stream. The air will ring with shouts of praise. The name of the gracious God will be on his lips as he takes the glad news to neighbors and friends.

Have you had that soul-changing experience? Have you taken your sins to Him and spread them forth in His sight? Have you confessed them all and begged with fervent prayers for cleansing and forgiveness and restoration? Has He come and taken your sins away, washing you thoroughly and giving you a new heart? Has He set the bells of joy ringing again in your soul? If all these things have happened in you and if this is your experience, why not break forth with songs and shout praises to Him? Why not be the happiest person on the earth? Why not *teach transgressors* His *ways* so that *sinners may be converted unto Him*? A significant verse in Acts (5:42) reveals the secret of the unparalleled success of the early Christians who had found such joy. Luke tells us: *And daily in the temple, and in every house, they ceased not to teach and preach Jesus Christ.* What will happen in your church and in mine if we go forth with the heartening testimony until every neighbor has heard our word concerning His saving grace? Do you know Him? Has He forgiven your sins? Are you a new creature in Him? Are you rejoicing in your soul because of the priceless gift you have received from Him? Can you afford to let David be more joyous or more effective than you? Will lost men and women spend eternity in hell simply because you sealed up the good news and refused to carry the message to others? May this psalm speak its message to our own cold hearts and then through us to a sinning world. He who is eager to pardon, strong to save and ready to guide can transform the lives of those to whom we go. May courage and compulsion be given to us as we recognize the urgency of the matter. It is later than you think.

> O safe to the Rock that is higher than I,
> My soul in its conflicts and sorrows would fly;
> So sinful, so weary, Thine, thine would I be;
> Thou blest "Rock of Ages," I'm hiding in Thee.

III

FROM DOUBT TO CERTAINTY

PSALM 73

Surely God is good to Israel, even to such as are of a clean heart. But as for me, my feet were almost gone; my steps had well-nigh slipped. For I was envious at the foolish, when I saw the prosperity of the wicked. For there are no bands in their death; they are not in trouble as other men. Their eyes stand out with fatness; they have more than heart could wish. And they say, How does God know? And is there knowledge in the Most High? Behold, these are the ungodly, who prosper in the world; they increase in riches. . . . Surely I have cleansed my heart in vain, and washed my hands in innocency. For all the day long have I been plagued, and chastened every morning. . . . When I thought to know this, it was too painful for me, until I went into the sanctuary of God; then understood I their end. Surely thou didst set, them in slippery places; thou didst cast them down into destruction. How are they brought into desolation, as in a moment! They are utterly consumed with terrors. . . . Nevertheless I am continually with thee; thou dost hold me by my right hand. Thou wilt guide me with thy counsel, and afterward receive me to glory. Whom have I in heaven but thee? There is none upon earth that I desire besides thee.

WOULD you look with me upon the face of a man who is radiantly happy in the certainty that God is good and that life is filled to the brim with good things? His face beams with a strange radiance. There is a light in his eyes. He has found God and has felt a rich blessing flooding his soul. Doubt and fear and confusion have gone out the window. There is something contagious about his enthusiastic confidence. It will help us to find out from him the secret. We need to know how to be so certain of vital matters.

We find him quite willing to share with us the spiritual biography. It is a thrilling story of experiences that involved temptation, pitfalls, self-pity, disappointment, envy, doubt, and near disaster. He tells of the moment when he was on the very verge of an unspeakable calamity. He felt his feet going out from under him and the foundations on which he had depended crumbling. His faith was almost gone. Perhaps no one of us is able to realize the tragedy contained in that description. You would be alarmed to find that you were on the point of losing your hearing or your sight or your health. If the physician announced such disastrous news to you it would be almost more than you could bear. What about the realization that your faith is slipping away, that the grip on God is about gone, that you are losing the assurance of God's mercy and love and saving power? How would you react? Is it a matter of concern?

The psalmist, with unusual daring, pulls back the curtain and shows us the soul struggle that almost took him over the brink of the falls. We can watch him as he suffers under the cruel grip of doubt and envy and then see him as he turns to the one solution of his problem. At the end he lifts us up to the plane where we can not only rejoice with him but find the source of light and joy and assurance. The wreck into which he almost plunged is a disaster that all of us need to shun. The pitfalls are yawning before us. The confidence and certainty and joy which he found are possible for all of us. How may we become the possessors of such a faith? How may we avoid the perils that he missed? What is the secret?

We shall look first at his problems (1-14) and then at the solution (15-28).

In this gripping story we see God sitting by, quietly listening to the wild, unfair, angry talk of one who insisted on giving utterance to the deep envy of his hot soul. God, knowing that he would be ashamed of himself, let him talk on until he had poured forth all the perilous stuff that had produced his malady. How patient God is! We would be up and about the task of answering such charges. The psalmist prattled on about his neighbors and their prosperity, their wickedness, their false pride, their open blasphemy, their health and immunity from either sickness or sorrow or disappointment. He quit going to church and nursed his grievances day by day as his soul became soured. His morbid brooding gave envy an opportunity to get firm root in his mind. As he saw it life was filled with inequalities. While he and his family endured illnesses and poverty and loneliness his wicked neighbors enjoyed luxury and excellent health. These men who gave no thought to God prospered amazingly. No want of theirs was unsatisfied. They grew richer and richer. They were strong and healthy. Their characters were warped. Pride and selfishness ruled in all their behavior. Every time the psalmist thought of these men he was swept a step nearer apostasy. He became more certain that God was failing in His task of ordering the affairs of men. God was either asleep or uninterested or lacking in the proper regard for righteous standards or was unwilling to rule His creatures as justice demanded. Faith could not hope to stand in such an atmosphere. Self-pity came in and took possession. Envy grew by leaps and bounds. Bitterness had its inning. It goes without saying that the psalmist was miserable. His family must have suffered with him for he could not help make the home atmosphere what it needed to be. When one is out of tune with God he is not in position to bring happiness and contentment to others. We shudder to think of the unhappy situation in his home as he writhed in the throes of envy and self-pity.

As envy grew it was quite natural for him to ask, "Why be good? What is the use of the kind of loyalty that I used to have? Have I cleansed my heart in vain?" He was not in position to answer such questions. His perspective was bad. His conclusions must be wrong. He was on the very point of surrendering his faith. The foundations for his faith were giving way. No one would want to worship a God who was undependable. Something must have happened to show the miserable man the danger of his position. He realized that his faith was almost gone and that soon he would be a godless creature without hope or stay or anchor or God. Fortunately he became aware of the necessity for a decision. How could he solve his problem? What was he to do? Should he renounce God, peddle his doubts, go the way of the cynic, or go into the sanctuary to give God a chance to reclaim him? What would you do? Do you think you are as wise as this psalmist proved to be?

The psalmist tells us that he ran into the sanctuary for the solution. He put himself where God could deal with him. Realizing his own helplessness he turned to the holy place where the Great Physician could be found for diagnosis and healing. He found himself strangely steadied by the mysterious power of the holy place. Memories of other days flooded his mind. How near God had been in those days! What joys he had known! How rich had been the fellowship in this sacred place! Strangely enough he felt that God knew he was there and was making His way to him. It warmed his heart to know that his God was singling him out for a special revelation. He tells us nothing of the furnishings, the choir, the sermon, or the program of worship. Do you think a seeking stranger could be as conscious of God's presence if he came to your church next Sunday? This poor fellow found God and knew that God was vitally interested in him and his problem. He realized that God was working out a special demonstration that would solve his problem. How easy it would be for many of our distraught people to find the solution to their problems in the sanctuary!

As he sat reverently in the place of worship a new panorama was unfolded before his eyes. In some mysterious way he was enabled to see his wicked neighbors in their true light. These men who had seemed to be so prosperous, so carefree, so happy, were now pictured in dangerous waters. Fears, disquietude, hidden yearnings, unsatisfied desires, and cankering sores showed up in glaring reality as God's picture opened before him. Their triumphs and their prosperity are temporary. Their outward manifestations of contentment but cover a heart filled with unsatisfied longings. Terrifying perils surround them. Feverish fears and anxieties paralyze them. Thirsts and hungers that hitherto had been unobserved are clearly evident in their hearts and lives.

Suddenly the psalmist catches his breath as he looks upon the certain destruction that awaits them down the road. They are rushing blindly and madly toward a fearful end. Prosperity at best is but a passing and temporary thing. The strong hand of a righteous God is in full control and will bring about the certain destruction for those who have left Him out of their hearts. Why be envious of wicked men? Why begrudge them the fleeting pleasures that come their way in life's brief stay? Why lose faith in God because of the passing prosperity of men who are about to be plunged into miseries unspeakable? In a moment he saw his own folly, his own foolish heart, his own shallow conception of what is really important in life. He saw that he had greatly exaggerated the things that these godless men had enjoyed. They had no inner wealth. They knew no genuine joys. They possessed nothing that would last. They had no anchor for the approaching storm. They had no God. Sudden destruction was near. The inevitable crash must engulf them. It is a stupid man who envies the godless man the little that his poor mind enjoys. Let us remember that it was in the sanctuary that the poor stumbling man found this divinely-given truth.

Suddenly and without warning the worshiper saw himself on the screen before him. He was rather startled for he had not contemplated such an opportunity. He found to his amazement that he was in possession of great wealth. He realized that he was constantly in the very presence of his God. No one could estimate what a treasure he had. *I am continually with thee.* What a store of riches that line uncovers! All through his days of misery and envy and doubt he has had the eternal God near him. He has been near to protect him, to sustain and nourish and keep him, to point the way at every crossroad, to drive fear away when danger and uncertainty sought to overwhelm him, to bind up and heal and restore him in hours of pain and distress and exhaustion, to fill all the days and all the nights with a calm assurance and a steady faith, to give sweet fellowship when loneliness threatened, to set the joybells ringing in his heart when it seemed all music had fled, to provide the needed courage and strength to undertake the impossible in the realization that underneath are the everlasting arms. In shadow, in sunshine; in work, in play; in tears, in joy; in youth, in old age; in life, in the hour of death, the poet realizes that he has the continual touch of a loving God as the source of uncounted, unfailing wealth. He has been with him all the way and he did not realize it.

No sense of the full meaning of the divine presence had ever entered his mind. He now sees that all the money, all the prosperity, all the success and popularity, could never bring such blessings to godless men. He now knows that **God** is near to help, ready to hold his right hand, willing to guide every step, able to supply every need of the journey, anxious to satisfy every thirst and every hunger of his soul. One day He will welcome him into the beautiful home at the end of the way. No wonder he says, *Whom have I in heaven but thee? There is none upon the earth that I desire besides thee. . . . God is the strength of my heart, and my portion forever. . . . It is good for me to draw near to God. I have put my trust in the Lord God, that I may declare all thy works.* He is overwhelmed with a tremendous conviction of God's marvelous goodness. He is still just as poor, just as far from earthly prosperity and popularity, but he is going back into life with a new inward possession. He has God! God's gracious nearness, His supporting grasp, His unfailing counsel, His directing finger, His royal welcome into the heavenly home, are opened up to the mind of the worshiper as he lets God teach him. Confidence has broken in on his soul. He is no longer envious. Instead of ugly self-pity he has genuine compassion for the poor godless ones who stumble on without such matchless treasures, instead of doubt he has a faith that is clear as the sunlight, instead of gloom and sadness he has ringing joybells in his heart, instead of complaint he has jubilant praise and unrestrained thanksgiving. Faith has climbed through struggle to higher ground as the soul has been open before the wooing call of a loving Father. He has a firm hold on the reality out of which the doctrine of the resurrection can easily grow. He knows that he will be in God's hand. Knowing Him as he has now come to know Him, he is certain that he will be safe in this world and forever. Such assurance is born in the crucible of God's own presence. Surely he was created to walk with God and to continue in God's presence throughout eternity. It was the victory of religous experience. He realized that he was in the

shadow of God's love and care. We can almost hear him say
with Whittier:

> I know not where His islands lift
> Their fronded palms in air;
> I only know I cannot drift
> Beyond His love and care.

Nothing can now separate him from the love of God. We
wish we might give him a copy of Paul's triumphant message
in the eighth chapter of Romans. The love that refused to
let go will keep him in the intimacy of God's presence. He
knows God's message for a troubled heart. Confusion and
frustration cannot bring distress to his soul. He has arrived
at a settled faith that will prove an anchor through all the
days ahead.

Is your soul torn with confusion? Have you lost your grip
on God? Has your soul become embittered by pain, discouragement, loneliness, fear, or doubt? Are you in danger
of losing your footing, your faith, your courage in the slippery way? Would you seek a remedy? Would you welcome
the individual treatment that God stands ready to give to
those who seek Him? Why not turn to the sanctuary? Have
you lost your touch with His holy place? Why not come back
and put yourself in the atmosphere where God can give you
a clear picture of His loving heart?

You may be certain that an answer awaits you in the sanctuary. Something happens there. If life is demanding more
than your weary soul can bear; if you feel yourself crushed
under life's cruel blows; if self-pity, bitterness, envy, and
cynicism reach for the controls of your better self, run eagerly to some sanctuary of God. You will find Him there. You
will be thrilled to know that He has an individual welcome
for you. His voice will speak to your heart. Your problem
can be spread out before One who is a loving Father. You

will be blessed by His words: *My grace is sufficient for thee.*
What a blessed assurance! In the house dedicated to the worship of God, weary hearts have found a strength, a solace, a
blessing that no words can describe.

Eddie Cantor tells of an experience in one of our largest
cities. Without warning a terrific wind swept through the
city, accompanied by a blinding rain. Along with many
others Mr. Cantor found himself crouching in the huge, shel-
tering doorway of a church. His words to us carry a much
needed lesson: "The world today is going through something
far more threatening than a windstorm. Every single one of
us needs refuge of one kind or another. I know of no better
place to go for it than a church. The greatest calamity that
can befall a people is the loss of religion. Don't let it happen here. Go to church."

In His sanctuary you will find God. You will be conscious
of His deep interest in you and your problems and your
faith. You will be thrilled by the thought that you have the
constant presence of God in every moment of your life. *Lo,
I am with you always.* You will be lifted out of fear and
doubt and discouragement and despair by the undergirding
arms about you, keeping you in all your journey. You will
be strengthened by the assurance that you are to enjoy true
guidance as your feet reach out into the unknown way.

In the darkest hour you can feel the strong hand of the
Guide directing your steps. How can you fear? How can you
miss the way? The keenest realization of all will come to your
soul in the knowledge that He is directing your steps into
the eternal home already prepared for you at the end of the
journey. No joy could ever be richer than yours when you
see and understand the full import of that assurance. He has
gone to prepare a place for you. He is coming again to receive you unto Himself and into that eternal home where

joys unspeakable will be yours throughout the endless ages of eternity.

Are not these the very assurances that your heart craves? Can you compare these treasures with all the things the world can offer? A loving Father wants to give you the golden certainty of these riches. Will you surrender your will to Him, and let the sunlight of certainty flood your soul? You will find Him in the sanctuary.

IV

VOLUNTEERS

PSALM 110

The Lord said to my Lord, Sit thou at my right hand, until I make thine enemies thy footstool. The Lord will send the rod of thy strength out of Zion. Rule thou in the midst of thine enemies. Thy people are free-will offerings in the day of thy power, in the beauties of holiness; from the womb of the morning thou hast the dew of thy youth. The Lord has sworn, and will not repent, Thou art a priest forever after the order of Melchizedek.

ALL the world loves a volunteer. The heart is strangely stirred by the spectacle of a young adventurous spirit that dares step out and take upon himself some dangerous assignment. The author of this psalm has presented a king who is also a priest who volunteers to be the leader in a deadly encounter with a cruel foe. It is a battle unto the death. It is to end in victory for the Volunteer. In the same beautiful poem is the picture of a multitude of youthful warriors streaming forward to take their places as near the Leader as possible as He rushes forth to the battle. They are volunteers. The drama is packed with color and vividness. The death struggle involves many brave young warriors who seem to be born for this titanic engagement.

In these introductory statements let us say that we regard these words as words of David referring directly to the Messiah and His work in wresting God's created sons from the power of the devil. David is, in this psalm, a prophet of God and predicts the career and victory of the Messiah, the Son of God. In our humble opinion it does not refer to any earthly king but to the Messiah alone. No human being could possibly fill this picture. In the fullness of time the Messiah came as the Babe of Bethlehem to take up His active campaign against the devil. Without embarrassment we shall recognize Him as the Priest-King of this poem and study it on that basis. No psalm is more frequently quoted in the New Testament. Our Lord used it in a remarkable way in His conversation with the Pharisees, Scribes and Sadducees.

The King Volunteers

In the poetic setting the Messiah is presented as seated at the right hand of the Father in the divine throne room. With all His kingly dignity He is ready to shoulder His part of the responsibility to redeem and restore lost humanity to its former place of glory and dignity. He has been chosen by His Father to rule. He has also received from the hand of His Father the prerogatives of the priestly office. He is not to be made a priest because of his birth in the hereditary line, but by divine appointment **He becomes *a priest forever after the order of Melchizedek*.** While we look upon Him He is gazing longingly at the lost creatures of the earth under the power of the evil one. In His heart there is a consuming love for lost men and a great yearning to see the power of the devil broken so that men may come back to the Father's house. The divine decree assures Him of victory over the fanatical foe. Suddenly He announces His intention to go forth as a Warrior to break the devil's power and free the captives. In His eyes can be seen a great, burning passion to save. He loves lost and enslaved men. He will go forth to save them. He dedicates Himself to the task of redeeming lost men. The Volunteer is ready to devote Himself as an offering. He looks about Him for soldiers who will be members of His army to give battle to the kingdom of evil. It is a tense moment. Who will make up the army? Shall He go forth alone? Can He hope to have soldiers who are imbued with the same high purpose and committed to the same holy cause?

EAGER VOLUNTEERS

The heart of the King is cheered by the spontaneous response and the joyful recognition accorded Him. No king has ever witnessed such instant loyalty and devotion. In some strange way the eager young men have been able to understand the mysterious challenge of the cause to which He has devoted His life. They have sensed the fact that this noble King has set Himself to enter the great Armageddon that will guarantee the final defeat for the forces of unrighteousness. They can see the danger, the sacrifice, the crucial struggle, the death wounds, but the certainty of victory thrills their very souls. They have fallen desperately in love with their Leader and no sacrifice is too much to make for Him. Such a cause demands the deepest loyalty and the costliest sacrifice. He shall not go into battle alone. The life and death struggle will find them in the thick of the fighting. They are ready to go.

Thy people offer themselves willingly in the day of thy muster. The assurance is given that conscription or pressure will not be necessary. The battle must have multitudes of strong human helpers but they are already responding. With eagerness and alacrity they rush forward to prostrate themselves before Him and take the oath of loyalty. The poet has given a beautiful touch to the picture in his use of the noun instead of the verb. He is literally saying, *Thy people shall be free-will offerings.* Each of them comes in a burst of enthusiastic devotion to lay his body on the altar in front of the King as a votive offering. The spirit is the same as that evidenced by Abraham when he bound his only son, Isaac, and laid his body on the altar in response to the command of God. When the cruel knife was raised to shed his blood as an offering to God Abraham proved his love for, and his devotion to, his divine Lord. These young volunteers come in that same spirit and with that same surrender to devote their last ounce of energy and the last drop of blood to prove their love for their King. It is a glad, spontaneous sacrifice of all to the One who richly deserves their all. We are reminded of the response of the people in Deborah's day when the governors of Israel *offered themselves willingly.* In this picture the King is assured that His army will be made up of willing followers who love Him and who will not refuse Him the last breath if it is needed to bring victory. Paul states the New Testament version: *I beseech you therefore, brethren, by the mercies of God, that ye present your bodies a living sacrifice, holy, acceptable unto God, which is your reasonable service. And be not conformed to this world, but be ye transformed by the renewing of your mind, that ye may prove what is that good, and acceptable, and perfect will of God.*

Another note indicates that these volunteers are young and vigorous and venturesome. They have not grown old enough to be ruled by caution and by fears. They are young enough to be good soldiers. Army officers do not want older men for the most perilous undertakings. Youth must be brought in to dare and risk and plunge forward into dangerous ventures. The king is thrilled by the thought that the youth of His realm will count it a sublime privilege to make up the army that is to go on the most dangerous mission ever undertaken. May it ever be true that our Lord may be able to count among His volunteers the young men and women who possess the brand of courage and daring that will make for victory. The youth of our day are the choice recruits for the force that is to storm the very gates of evil and help destroy all the kingdom of the devil. Isaiah tells us how we may find and keep eternal youth. *He giveth power to the faint; and to them that have no might he increaseth strength. Even the youths shall faint and be weary, and the young men shall utterly fall: But they that wait upon the Lord shall renew their strength; they shall mount up with wings as eagles; they shall run, and not be weary; and they shall walk, and not faint.*

Like their great Leader these young warriors are pictured as priests. The Messiah has as His one task the bringing of God and men together. His warfare is a holy struggle. The evil one must be destroyed along with his work. His subjects who are slaves must be persuaded to come back to the Creator for pardon and cleansing and the abundant life. In order to do this it will be necessary for Him to offer Himself as a sacrificial Substitute. His life must end in death that life may come to those who are held by sin's chains. These youthful warriors who press forward to dedicate themselves for the struggle unto death also accept the divinely-given office of priest. Their lives are devoted to the holy struggle that will bring men back to God. They are not only dedicated to die when necessary but they will engage in the heaven-directed work of saying to men, *Be ye reconciled to God.* They have the same spirit as their leader and will set their lives apart in full consecration to Him. As the Great High Priest offers Himself on the altar to save men they will offer their hearts to Him in holy living.

An additional note that catches our eye is the line, *in holy, beautiful garments.* How beautiful it is to see this magnificent multitude of marching men clothed in clean, fresh garments singing their songs of consecration! They have sensed the matchless purity of the Priest-King who leads, and have washed and scrubbed their garments until they glisten with whiteness in the early morning light. Isaiah said, *Be ye clean ye who bear the vessels of the Lord.* Thank God for young people who keep themselves clean for the Lord. In all generations we find those who "dare to be different" and who *purpose in their hearts that they will not defile themselves.* Happy is that church that has a group of young Christian soldiers who have kept themselves and their garments clean and are joyously walking with the Lord as He goes about His holy task of winning men back to the Father. The author of this psalm has painted an immortal picture of them. They are a holy band on urgent business for their Lord and King. With purity of heart and life they are on a great crusade. Their King calls to them as He moves triumphantly forward towards ultimate victory.

> Conquering now and still to conquer,
> Rideth a King in His might,
> Leading the hosts of all the faithful
> Into the midst of the fight;
> See them with courage advancing,
> Clad in their brilliant array
> Shouting the name of their Leader,
> Hear them exultingly say:
> Not to the strong is the battle,
> Not to the swift is the race
> Yet to the true and the faithful
> Vict'ry is promised through grace.

The reference to *dew* brings into the picture a beautiful touch that thrills all who read it. In that figure we see a symbol of the refreshing lift that this weary old world so sorely needs. David gives us a glimpse of the mysterious birth of the morning, so precious and so abundant in the dry Eastern lands. Along with the indescribable beauty of the dawn the poet remembers how the dew brings freshness and sparkle and new life to a dry, thirsty world. Suddenly he visualizes the weary, sin-cursed world awakened by the life-giving visit of One who is the *Water of Life*. He has been accompanied by multitudes of consecrated associates who have been given the power to distribute the refreshing, healing, nourishing dew in such quantities that all peoples know of their coming. He and His followers come to gladden, to freshen, to adorn, to make beautiful the dry, parched land and the dying hearts with the eternal freshness brought from *the womb of the morning*. These clean, consecrated young priestly warriors come as *dew* to the King. His spirits are lifted. He is refreshed and gladdened and prepared for His holy task. Their refreshing influence on others cannot be estimated. The gleaming beauty, the innumerable multitude, the priestly character, the wholehearted consecration, the flaming zeal, the burning eyes, the adoring love for their leader, and the joy visible in their very faces combine to cast a spell over those who see them. They are indeed *dew* in a needy world.

Jesus used the two figures *light* and *salt* to characterize the essential function of his ideal kingdom men. May we add this figure of *dew* and apply it to all our hearts? The salt is assigned the work of purifying and preserving. It must arrest and combat decay. The light has a more spectacular assignment of guiding and gladdening the hearts of those in the way. The dew freshens and fertilizes wherever it holds sway. Quietly, silently, unobserved it goes about its work of bringing freshness and life to a well-nigh exhausted world. It is God's will that His redeemed ones shall lose themselves in saving the world from rottenness and corruption and shine as lights in a darkened world and also spend themselves in refreshing and beautifying His world. It is a big assignment. Who is able to measure up? We have these qualities only as we keep close to Him and drink from His limitless fountain. We shall be effective as *salt*, as *light*, and as *dew* only as we are like Him in spirit, in character, in dedication to a cause, and in full surrender to do His will. How effective we need to be in a world where sin and darkness and death hold sway! The Messiah will be cheered today by that old word of assurance, *In holy garments, from the womb of the morning, thou hast the dew of thy youth.* How can you help to make it true? Isaiah said: *Here am I, send me.* Jeremiah gave his young heart to the Lord who called him to go against impossible odds. We are always strengthened by the assurances, *My grace is sufficient for thee* and *Lo, I am with you always.*

Throughout the psalm there is the note of unusual recklessness in disregarding self and plunging into the conflict. Reckless abandon is in evidence both in the behavior of the King and in the example of those who follow Him. No one counts his own life dear. No one hesitates when the cost is realized. Paul caught something of the idea when he speaks of Christ: *Let this mind be in you, which was also in Christ Jesus: Who, being in the form of God, thought it not robbery to be equal with God: But made himself of no reputation, and took upon him the form of a servant, and was made in the likeness of men: And being found in fashion as a man, he humbled himself, and became obedient unto death, even the death of the cross.* Such dedication to a cause brings certainty of victory. With high courage, strenuous effort, complete abandon, hearty obedience and overflowing joy the army moves forward singing their songs as they follow their beloved Leader. We rejoice today that many have qualified as loyal followers of His and are marching with Him.

> Onward, Christian soldiers,
> Marching as to war,

> With the cross of Jesus
> Going on before!
> Christ, the royal Master,
> Leads against the foe;
> Forward into battle,
> See, His banner go!

How may we become eligible for a place in His ranks? The cost is much bigger than one would suppose. The devil has helped make the price high. He has helped men place wrong price tags on so many things. Without thinking men have accepted the false values and have come to believe that certain things are of paramount importance. As long as this is true it will be almost impossible to interest one in paying the price for a place in that youthful army of singing soldiers. Jesus met such a man one day and did His best to rearrange the price tags so the young ruler could become one of the grandest members of that crusading group. With a sad heart he turned back into oblivion and misery when he had everything necessary to become a conquering associate of the King. Saul of Tarsus met Him one day after days and weeks of wrestling. In that Damascus Road experience the scholarly rabbi became the most powerful follower the King ever had.

Peter met Him one day and gladly gave up his few paltry hindrances to greatness and, under the challenging leadership of the King, became a valuable trophy of grace. Mary Magdalene came from a life of worthless pursuits to find the highest joys a soul can know and Jesus made her the first herald of the resurrection. A brilliant, young Greek Christian fell desperately in love with Jesus and gave himself so completely over to Him that martyrdom was a choice reward for him. The Holy Spirit gripped a young shoe clerk and so fired his soul that he gladly followed the example and the call of the Saviour he loved until evangelistic fires were kindled all over two continents. A young man by the name of George

Truett met and surrendered to his Lord and, under the divine hand, became his generation's most powerful voice for the spreading of the message of Christ. In England a thoughtful young cobbler learned of dying heathen souls who needed to hear the gospel and gladly gave his entire life to the holy crusade to India. Albert Schweitzer met and fell so desperately in love with Him that he turned away from a brilliant career in Europe as a doctor, a musician, a university professor, and an author, to go to darkest Africa to heal broken bodies and to help his Lord bring healing to dying souls. Eternity alone will reveal the influence of such consecrated men and women who have seen Him, fallen in love with Him, and given their lives in full surrender to him.

How may one become a marching crusader in this singing army? It is all your own work. Your will must be brought into play. No one else can force you or press you. A volunteer is the only one who can be admitted. You must first look upon Him and fall in love with Him and want to give yourself to Him. You must let your mind accept Him as your own personal Saviour and then you will have an uncontrollable desire to rush forward to give yourself wholly to Him. He will be the One person in all your thinking. He is the King, the High Priest, the Redeemer, the Sinless Substitute, the Saviour, and your Lord. You will not be able to hold yourself back from surrender to Him and to His cause when you see Him and His love and His zeal and His willingness to die that lost men may be saved. Through His eyes you will see lost men, miserable and lost, without a Saviour, heading toward an endless hell. You will be akin to Him so much by that time that you will be anxious to help save them. You will feel an imperial tug at your heart that you cannot resist. You will not be hindered by the fact that you have only a poor, insignificant life to offer. You will not hesitate because you consider the price too great. You will not turn away into shallowness and misery and selfishness when the divine King leads on to certain victory over sin and death and the fanatical foe who made it necessary for Jesus to die on the cross.

> See, from His head, His hands, His feet,
> Sorrow and love flow mingled down:
> Did e'er such love and sorrow meet,
> Or thorns compose so rich a crown?

In that blessed moment you will lay your trembling hand in His nail-pierced hand and pour out your own heart in thanksgiving to Him who became your Substitute. You will rejoice to lay your life in His keeping and rise to go forth as one of His shouting, singing, victorious, **crusading** army. You will find more joy to the square inch than you have ever known in all your days. Eternity alone can reveal the blessings that will come to the heart of the Saviour, to your own heart, and to the needy hearts that will be turned to Him because of your testimony. One day around the throne in the presence of the Father your happiness will reach heights too great for words. When you see this victorious One sweeping in with countless millions saved by His atoning death and unending seeking, you will then rejoice in the knowledge that you were a member of His army.

V

LIGHT IN A DARK NIGHT

PSALM 139

O Lord, thou hast searched me, and known me. Thou knowest my downsitting and my uprising; thou understandest my thought from afar. Thou compassest my path and my lying down, and art acquainted with all my ways. . . . Such knowledge is too wonderful for me; it is high, I cannot comprehend it. Whither shall I go from thy Spirit? Or whither shall I flee from thy presence? If I ascend into heaven, thou art there. If I make my bed in Sheol, behold, thou art there. If I take the wings of the morning, and dwell in the uttermost parts of the sea; even there shall thy hand lead me, and thy right hand shall hold me. . . . My frame was not hid from thee when I was made in secret, and curiously wrought in the lowest parts of the earth. . . . When I awake I am still with thee. . . . Search me, O God, and know my heart. Try me, and know my thoughts. And see if there be any wicked way in me, and lead me in the way everlasting.

Do you know that God is intimately acquainted with you? Are you deluded sufficiently to believe that in the midst of more than two billion people you are too insignificant to claim His individual thought? Would it help or frighten you to know that His eye is upon you morning, noon, and night? Suppose you could see His eye peering through the ceiling at you and could feel His hand literally upon your hand. What would such knowledge do to you? How long could fears continue to hinder your life? What hope could the tempter have that he might control your life to his own devilish ends? The psalmist is vividly conscious of the actual presence of God every moment of his life. There is no inch of the earth's surface where He is not available. He is conscious of every move His creatures make. What a sobering thought for all of us!

He Knows Me (1-6)

In the unexplored, unknown and unexplained world into which we are all plunging, it should help me tremendously to realize that He knows perfectly all of my weakness and strength, all of my thoughts and fears, all of my secret desires and holy aspirations, all of my needs, my lacks, my deeper yearnings. His perfect knowledge of my life and of my thoughts is a truth that delights my soul. *Thou hast searched me, and known me. . . . Thou understandest my thoughts afar off . . . and art acquainted with all my ways. . . . Such knowledge is too wonderful for me.* Everything connected with his whole being and his whole life is an open book to his God. How often do you convince yourself that no one knows some ugly thing in your life or your thoughts? It becomes a nightmare to you as you imagine that sooner or later some person will find it out. Shame or disgrace will be your portion. You literally dread the hour when men will know your secret. How much camouflage, make-up, veneer we use to keep our dark secrets! An ugly scar or an unsightly deformity or a horrible blemish is so carefully covered and concealed. A cloak of silence covers some uglier stain or scar. We just cannot afford to let the secret out. It will ruin us! Would it startle you to learn that the secret is already out? The neighbors may not know, but our gracious Father in heaven knows. He not only knows just how it looks now but He knows just how it all happened and just how you failed in the hour of testing. The whole black chapter is open before His eyes. No pretty veil of rationalization has obscured it. No mantle of forgetfulness has toned down its vivid hues. No sweet perfume has been sprayed on to rob it of hideous odors. He knows it all.

He knows the weak places in your being and the aims and purposes that you have had. He knows how hard you have tried and how heavy the burdens you have been forced to carry. He understands the handicaps that have kept you from reaching the goals you set for yourself. He also knows how miserably you have failed to live up to His standard for your life. He can sense the barrenness, the ignorance, the lost opportunities, the wasted years. He can count up the lost souls who will spend eternity in hell because you failed to tell them the story of saving grace. He knows, too, the many deeds of kindness and thoughtfulness that you have taken time out to do in His holy name. He can put your own little puny life up against His blueprint of your life and record all the differences. Yes, dear friend, He knows it all. He is able to use His own divine fluoroscope and look through all the veneer, the tinsel, the make-up, and the genuine. It hurts to know that our God is like this—and yet it helps, too, since we will be spurred to live bigger, richer, sweeter, nobler, more Christlike lives because of it. We will be encouraged to know that an all-wise and an all-knowing God will take account of some of the hidden riches and qualities that otherwise would be unnoticed and unrewarded. Thank God for the knowledge that He knows me!

He Is With Me (7-10)

The psalmist catches his breath with the startling realization that he cannot get away from God. He is swept with the thrilling thought that God is always near him. The "everywhereness" of God is a challenging thought and one that should give us pause, but our poet has hit upon a thought that is even more arresting. He is not trying to teach the fact that God is everywhere in all the earth. He is more vivid and personal in his presentation of the fact that God is with him personally everywhere he goes. There is an individual appropriation of the doctrine that lifts it instantly into a new realm. He has the thrilling consciousness that God is always with him. He says: *Whither shall I flee from thy presence? . . . If I take the wings of the morning, and dwell in the uttermost parts of the sea; even there shall thy hand lead me, and thy right hand shall hold me.*

In hours like these, it should help us to become aware of the presence of God. He comes to give courage and assurance and confidence for every difficult journey and for every task. In the dark watches of the night, mothers and fathers and wives may reach out to grip the hand of One who is always near and who always understands the deepest heart throbs. When the load becomes so heavy that the human frame cannot struggle any longer, the heart can gather new strength to carry on when it is clearly known that He is there. How much easier it is when we know He is there to help. When the tempter comes to lure us into sin, it is the consciousness of His presence by our side that guarantees victory. Who of us can do some foul deed when we look up to see His loving eyes upon us? What a powerful force to keep us clean and strong and make us victorious in our battles with the devil. Fears have no power over us when we know that He is in the room with us or walking by our side. Why should we let fear harm us when we look around to feel the close presence of the best Friend a man ever had? Loneliness loses its power to cause us to be miserable when we are cheered by His gracious presence. No wasting of time or loss of opportunity will mar the life that always looks up to see the divine Leader asking for our best efforts in helping those about us. No profane or hurtful word can escape our lips when we are aware that He is listening to every word that escapes our tongue. No unworthy thought can find place in our minds when we keep before us the realization that He knows every thought of every mind. No word of gossip or unfriendly criticism can slip from our tongue when we know how seriously He will be hurt by such a stab in the back. In short, it will make all the difference in our thoughts, our attitudes, our words, and in our deeds when we stop to realize that He is by our side. Linnaeus, a great botanist, had a motto carved in marble over the entrance to his laboratory: *Numen adest vivete innocui.* ("Live innocently. Do not sully hand and heart today. Deity is present.")

Adam tried to hide from God. Down through the ages his descendants have tried the same thing. Each of us imagines that it is possible to get out of His sight. Our psalmist declares in no uncertain terms that it is utterly impossible. It may be that you will go sailing along unmindful of His presence, but one day you will be shocked to find Him there. Will you be embarrassed to look up and find His eyes fixed upon you? Do you go to places where you hope He will not find you? Do you think thoughts that you hope He will never know? Our author plainly tells us that He is there, and that He does know. How will you adjust yourself to that disturbing declaration?

Another assurance that should bring peculiar delight is the promise he makes that our God will lead us. He helps us see that God not only knows and is continuously by our side, but that He leads us and holds our hand. In the dark maze of life with all its pits and dangers, he is cheered by the thought, *His hand shall lead me.* Guidance is the rich gift that comes from the divine hand. How sweet it is to know that the road to victory and usefulness and joy can be pointed out by the Good Shepherd who knows the way and leads us into the way of His own choosing. In that same verse, the poet says: *Thy right hand shall hold me.* What a soul-stirring thought it is to know that we are upheld and undergirded by the hand of the eternal God! In a day when all about us seems to be toppling and nothing is secure, it will surely help us to know that our own shaking hand is being held by the great right hand of God. He has a righteous purpose for each one of us and for His world that He has created. When our inner desires call out for security and safety, we are assured of His continued presence in our midst to bring order out of chaos and quiet confidence out of anxious turmoil. He assures us that *underneath are the everlasting arms.* He says: *Fear not, for I have redeemed thee, I have called thee by thy name; thou art mine. When thou passest through the waters, I will be with thee, and through the rivers, they shall not overflow thee; when thou walkest through the fire, thou shalt not be burned.* Our blessed Saviour said: *Lo, I am with you always even unto the end of the world.*

Each of us is strangely lured to the prow of the boat to set our eyes on the horizon. What does tomorrow hold for us? What is beyond the horizon? As a youth we ask the question, "Where? What? How? When?" The future is an unexplored land. Beautiful valleys, high mountains, shimmering landscapes, rolling seas, hidden rocks and howling storms lie before us. The psalmist would assure the impulsive youth that *God is there.* In thoughtful middle life we wonder about what lies ahead. Will it be danger or health or illness or success or frustration? Let us be certain of one definite assurance —*God is there.* In old age we shall ask the same question, "What is beyond the horizon? What shall I find?" As we round the curve or climb over the hill, we may be certain of one eternal assurance—*God is there.* Since He is to be there, we may be certain of a radiance, a beauty, a quiet confidence that only His presence can make possible.

Every one of us needs an unusual amount of courage and confidence in facing the future in hours like these. We can go into darkest clouds undergirded by the touch of His blessed hand. New burdens will give us an opportunity to test His mighty strength; new temptations will but demonstrate the effect of His pressure upon our arm; new fears will reveal His power in conquering fear. Each victory we win will make other victories possible. Each horizon we reach will give added assurance of new triumphs as other horizons loom before us. May we go with calm confidence and holy joy knowing always that *God is there*.

He Has Formed Me (13-18)

The psalmist is moved by the realization that God has a peculiar claim upon him because of the creative activity that brought him into being. The creator always has a right to make demands on the creature or the created thing. He is precious in God's sight because of the marvelous way he was created. He is a peculiar possession of the great Creator. With reverence and awe and sincere appreciation, he recounts God's mysterious creative activity. He knows that he is a special object of divine love. Surely we should be profoundly grateful to our dear Father God for all His manifold gifts to us. We owe a debt of gratitude that will forever mount up. Not only has He formed us, but He has ransomed us from horrible slavery at unbelievable cost. How we should love Him and serve Him! His great love for us should elicit from us the strongest love imaginable in return. Then His great purpose for us should challenge a devotion such as the world has not seen. So He has a right to demand our best love and devotion by right of creation, by right of redemption, by reason of His great love for us, and because of His eternal purpose for us.

> Were the whole realm of nature mine,
> That were a present far too small;
> Love so amazing, so divine,
> Demands my soul, my life, my all.

As a consequence, the psalmist gives utterance to a beautiful prayer. Listen to him as he says: *Search me, O God, and know my heart; try me, and know my thoughts; and see if there be any wicked way in me, and lead me in the way everlasting.* In the light of all that has been said in the earlier part of the psalm, it is all the more significant that he should close his poem with an earnest invitation to come in for a close and thorough examination of mind and heart and motive. He wants the divine Examiner to use the most powerful X-ray apparatus to detect the slightest beginnings in the direction of sin. He wants no corner left concealed. He wants to know the worst and know it quickly. He has faith in the Great Physician and does not hesitate to call for the full diagnosis. It is his one opportunity to secure the verdict on his inner heart. It is implied that he will be willing to have the Surgeon who makes the diagnosis go in with the knife to cut out and remove forever the evidences of "wicked ways" that He finds there. He wants no malignant growths to get firm root in his heart.

It would be a great day in our lives if we could come to think of God as this psalmist pictured Him and then, after full contemplation, call Him in for the examination and the surgery so sorely needed. Stop where you are and let the consciousness that God knows all about you sink into your inner mind. He knows your thoughts, your desires, your yearnings, your secret imaginations, your incipient rebellions and sins, your noble aims and purposes. He knows the way, the hills, the valleys, the traps, the springs. He not only knows you, but He has set Himself to go with you every step of that way. Your business life, your social engagements, your home experiences, lonely hours, heavy-loaded days, are all open to Him. Nothing is hidden from Him. You will not be able to give Him the slip and dart away on some secret escapade. He will be there all the way. Every minute is to be lived in His presence.

In addition to these two sobering thoughts, let your mind turn to the thought that you are really a special creation of the divine hand. It dignifies personality to know that one is the direct and individual creation of His blessed hand. Your body is created in the image of God and in His likeness to be a special home for the Holy Spirit to live. What a sanctity hovers over your body, mind, and spirit when you get this conception of the creative work of God's fingers. In the light of all this thought-provoking logic, what manner of man ought you to be? Why not fall on your knees as the psalmist did and say: *Search me . . . try me . . . see . . . lead me?* It could well be a grand day of beginning again for you. It might require painful surgery, days of hospitalization, and even a radical change in your manner of life, but you will find more joy to the square inch than you have ever known, a release from the fears and prodding of the conscience, a new surge of clean lifeblood in your whole being, an evidence of new fruit that will delight your heart, and a thrilling consciousness that you are walking with Him here, and that you will live with Him throughout the endless ages of eternity.

VI
MAKING JOYBELLS RING

Who passing through the valley of Baca make it a place of fountains. . . . They go from strength to strength. . . . O Lord of hosts, blessed is the man who trusts thee.

For what do you live? How much does your presence in the world mean to others? As you journey through life what influences are set in motion that gladden the hearts of others and make life brighter? In a world where irritations, frustrations, tragedies, heartaches, poverty, poor health, handicaps, unhappy home conditions, and cruel loneliness are so universally evident, how do you fit into the picture? Your general direction is good. You steer a clear, strong course toward a worthy goal at the end of the way but how are you contributing to the lives of those who may be fortunate enough to meet you on the way? You abstain from ugly crimes and sins with exceptional strength of character. You drive yourself in the pursuit of the full realization of a big life purpose but are you conscious of the innumerable hearts that appear along the way, hungry for a lift, ready to break under the load, confused and honestly seeking the way home? The message from the heart of this psalm should grip your heart and change your life.

THE BACKGROUND

The psalmist is a lonely soul who lives (for the time being at least) in some distant land where he finds himself shut off from God's holy house and its worship. He is an ardent and devoted lover of the Temple. Just as in Psalms 42 and 43 he pictures something of the tragic misery one suffers when he is denied access to the sanctuary and the worship of God. He writes for us a hymn of the divine life in all ages. In it we are brought face to face with the grace and the glory of divine worship where God alone can supply the inner heart with its resources of joy and fellowship and enrichment.

In the three stanzas he tells us of: the longing of the heart for God's sanctuary, and the joy and privilege of those who dwell there (1-4); the thrill of overcoming difficulties to stand in that holy place of worship (5-8); the precious privilege which God gives to those who trust Him and worship in His holy place (9-12). A full study of these stanzas would be helpful but we shall turn to the thought in verse six to form the basis of our study.

The author who has suffered under enforced absence from the sanctuary imagines himself in the midst of the throng of pilgrims who make their way over the long route to the place of worship. He is transported into extravagant thinking as he sees these friends making their way over hill and plain and valley, day after day, happy in the companionship of one another, "going from strength to strength," until every one of them stands in the presence of the God in Zion.

THE SERMON

It is in this beautiful picture that he gives us the text: *passing through the vale of Baca they make it a place of springs*. The word "Baca" is derived from the verb "weep." It can be translated "weeping" and would give us the idea that these pilgrims passing through groups of sorrow-laden people were able to change the tears into gladness. Kirkpatrick would not use the word "weeping" but prefers keeping the word "Baca" and interpreting it as "some waterless and barren valley through which pilgrims passed on their way to Jerusalem, but faith turns it into a place of springs, finding refreshment under the most untoward circumstances, while God refreshes them with showers of blessings from above, as the autumnal rains clothe the dry plains with grass and flowers." Either way we translate it we find the same clear message for our own hearts. Just as the rains come to a dry, barren desert to transform it from a scene of death into a lovely garden, or a radiant personality with a song and a smile comes into a tear-laden group, changing tears into smiles and sobs into songs, even so may we who have Christ in our hearts make a genuine contribution while we are "passing through." Instead of leaving fainting pilgrims we leave marching singers whose songs have been set going because of the presence of the one who "passed by."

Do you realize that a large part of your life is made up of necessary "passing through" unattractive places on our way to the place of work or worship? Every day finds us on our way to and from certain rather important places. When your family gets in the car to go to California one of the topics of conversation is the desert. A hot, blistering, barren, unattractive stretch of miserable travel awaits each traveler. How will you be able to cross from Needles to Barstow or from Blythe to Banning? Going and coming this stretch of desert is a necessary evil. One could wish for a push button that could eliminate this dreary part of the journey. No one relishes the thought of those dreary miles but everyone must make his way through them if he is to enjoy the beauties of the paradise beyond.

These pilgrims find themselves on their way to a highly

desired spot but in their going they have within their own
hearts just what it takes to transform the desert into a lovely
garden. They not only can endure the *vale of weeping* without losing heart but they re-create it into a joyous place of
songs. God is so real to them, their religion is so vital, their
joy is so genuine, their faces are so radiant, their songs are
so uplifting, their spirit is so contagious, that their "passing
through" makes a difference.

What is life doing to you? When you come in contact with
disease, temptations, disasters, disappointments, and heartaches what happens? The smart young student complained
of the wicked world God had made and said that he was
sure he could make a better one. A wise pastor reminded him
that the way was open and that God had put him into the
world for that very purpose. God would have you turn your
own valley into a place of refreshing springs where not only
your own soul but the souls of all your neighbors may be
refreshed and revived and made to sing aloud of His mercy.

You know the power and speed of the matchless Glenn
Cunningham but do you know how he came to be the best
mile runner in the world? When a child he was badly burned
in a schoolhouse fire. The doctors despaired of his life. They
openly declared that he would never be able to walk. What
a tragic situation! How adjust oneself to such a blow? Watch
the youngster as he heroically held on to the handles of the
plow and literally forced his badly crippled legs to respond.
Months and years of pain and punishment brought victory
and Glenn became the proud possessor of the fastest legs in
the whole world. He refused to let the *vale of Baca* hold him
down to its blueprint for his life. He succeeded in effecting a
marvelous change in the program that seemed to be set up
for him.

John Bunyan was not pleased with the Bedford jail. No one
could like such a place. He could have written a book reveal-

ing self-pity, bitterness, complaining and despair. His sensitive soul was sorely hurt by all the circumstances that surrounded him. It was truly a *valley of Baca*. He made it a literal fountain of rich, satisfying, soul-filling blessings for men of all races and all ages. Eternity alone can reveal the treasures planted in millions of minds by the immortal author of *Pilgrim's Progress*. He refused to let that *vale of Baca* cheat him of golden opportunities.

Florence Nightingale, with wealth and ease and luxuries and countless friends, discovered a vale laden with groans and germs and fever and gangrene and stark despair and certain death. She could have kept her place in English society and lived in quiet disregard of the impossible vale of suffering in the Crimea. How could she be held responsible for the tragic situation among the men of the army? Instead she used her money, her time, her strength, her radiant smile, her deep sympathy, her sacrificial spirit, to transform the ugliest *vale of Baca* into a place where grateful hearts poured out genuine gratitude for one who had so perfectly demonstrated an unselfish love. Eternity alone will reveal the incredible contribution of the Angel of the Crimea. As long as time stands men will sing her praises and thank God for one who blazed a trail for the feet of countless thousands who have dedicated themselves to heal humanity's hurts.

Paul, after persecutions, beatings, sufferings, and false accusations, found himself in a prison that was far worse than any modern jail. In that Roman prison he went about the glorious task of transforming his *vale of Baca* into a springing fountain that pours forth healing streams to hungry hearts and thirsty beings. His great letter to the Philippians breathes the air of the celestial hills of God rather than the damp, doleful, death-dealing fumes of a rat-infested prison. Not only was his own spirit lifted and made sweet but he was able to bless those who visited him and those who have read and will read his matchless words.

Phillips Brooks was one of America's greatest preachers. His place as king in the pulpit was unquestioned. Boston knew him as a mighty prophet of God. One day in the leading New England paper there appeared the following line which speaks for itself: "Yesterday opened cloudy and unpleasant; but about noon Phillips Brooks came downtown, and everything brightened up." Do you see it? Just one man walked down the street in a darkened city. What a powerful influence such a man can have! What is your status in this matter? Do you tend in that direction? When you walk through a street does it help?

Robert Browning, in one of his immortal classics, pictures for us the transforming effect of a little girl whose name is Pippa. On her walk to the factory she makes her way through a street where disappointment and defeat and despair are the dominant notes. Sadness and sorrow reign. When Pippa passes all is different. Every house on the street feels the effect of her song and her radiant personality. She sings because there is a glad song in her heart. Passing through she lifts drooping hearts, cheers the very atmosphere of a drab neighborhood until joybells are ringing all around. Why not? Is this not the very heart of Christianity? Pippa is happier. Everybody else is happier. Why not replace a sob with a song?

In Christ's teachings He recorded for us an unforgettable picture of a man we call the good Samaritan. How was it that this principle was taught in His story? The unfortunate man who lay by the roadside, wounded, bleeding, dying, provided the occasion. Along came a priest whose engagement in Jericho or in Jerusalem made it necessary for him to travel that lonely road. Passing along he could have proved a friend to the stranger by the way. Instead he was too intent on the duties at the end of the journey to pay attention to one in distress. *He passed by on the other side*. The Levite, traveling the same road, soon came face to face with the same opportunity and demonstrated the same unwillingness to be a friend. He *looked upon him, and passed by on the other side*. The Samaritan faced the unattractive road, the bleeding man, the need to hurry along to attend to his duties at the city. We are told that *he had compassion, and went to him, and bound up his wounds, and set him on his beast, and brought him to an inn, and took care of him*. He literally put into deed the inner teaching of our text. "Passing through" the despised road he made room for life-changing blessings. It was Jesus who taught this. The quality of soul that prompts such behavior is the very essence of His requirements for all who claim Him as Lord and seek to live by His words. In all of your travels in the pursuit of the goals to which you have set yourself how do you measure up to opportunities that present themselves by the way? How do you affect the *vale of Baca* when you pass through? Are you more like the priest or the Levite or the good Samaritan?

How did Jesus put into practice His high teachings on this subject? During His three years of teaching and healing and preparing men to assume the responsibility for carrying on His work how did he behave in the *vales of Baca*? The instances are too numerous to receive full mention. He always made a difference when he walked through any neighborhood. It was as He walked along on his way to some important engagement that he paused by the side of the road to heal blind Bartimaeus and to call Zacchaeus out of the tree to become a new creature. These two men were opportunities by the road as he was passing by. Mary Magdalene and Simon Peter and the rich young ruler were available trophies as he traveled. The young man kept his rebellious will in the way but Jesus gave His best in the appeal to him.

Perhaps the clearest New Testament illustration of our

text is the visit to Jacob's well. We are told that *He must needs pass through Samaria*. No one wanted to go that way. It was a necessity. How was it to be encountered? He was in Jerusalem. He wanted to get to Galilee. Samaria was in between. How did Jesus respond to this undesirable requirement? He took full advantage of one of the greatest opportunities ever presented to Him, and soon a sinful woman was made a new creature and her village was lifted out of sin and despair and soul hunger and death into a new citadel of rejoicing. What a blessed experience it was! Instead of a barren journey through one of earth's most hopeless *vales of Baca* they all witnessed the most sublime picture of the abounding grace of God in action. The eternal Son of God transformed the sinful town of Samaria into a lovely colony of heaven. Immortal souls were saved and made ready for eternity.

THE APPLICATION

You are vitally interested. You are willing to ask the psalmist to give you the recipe for such living. It seems almost too good to be true. You realize you are to travel this way but once and you honestly want to know the secret. The author points us to the context and asks us to read: *Blessed are they that dwell in thy house. . . . Blessed is the man whose strength is in thee. . . . Blessed is the man who trusteth in thee*. One who hopes to live like this must be in close touch with God. By prayer and sincere worship he must know how God thinks and loves and acts. Some of that divine compassion and that concern must be a vital part of his thinking. Just as Pippa blessed others as a natural expression of something that was deep in her own heart just so must he give forth from the bubbling fountain in his heart. To bless other lives as one passes is as unforced, as uncalculated and as unconscious as the perfume of a fragrant flower. It is because of a profound faith in God that the inner resources of one's soul are fed both to provide strength for victorious living and to send out streams to revive and to refresh those who need such vital necessities.

The real secret that must be saved to the last and emphasized is that Christ in your heart makes the difference. All the good resolutions, the fair promises, the conscious effort, the pressure of will and purpose, cannot avail until Christ becomes the controlling power in your heart and life. After all it is a Christlike grace that He alone can impart. When He lives in you and when you catch His spirit, and when that spirit gains control over your affections and your attitudes and your motives, the victory will come naturally. Heart and soul and voice and manner will be His so completely that men will see Christ in you. Paul says: *And all of us, with unveiled faces, reflecting like bright mirrors the glory of the Lord, are being transformed into the same likeness, from one degree of radiant holiness to another, even as derived from the Lord the Spirit* (Weymouth's translation). Just as the boy who spent so much time and devotion looking upon the Great Stone Face that he came to bear the very image in his face so will we who let His spirit dominate every thought and affection of our hearts, be effective in brightening sad hearts, arousing faith in God, helping in moments of decision, and starting anew in barren hearts the sound of joybells. He wants us to show forth the spirit of Christ in every day, in every road, in every contact. What will be your answer?

> While passing thro' this world of sin,
> And others your life shall view,
> Be clean and pure without, within,
> Let others see Jesus in you.
>
> Your life's a book before their eyes,
> They're reading it thro' and thro';

Say, does it point them to the skies,
Do others see Jesus in you?

Let others see Jesus in you,
Let others see Jesus in you;
Keep telling the story, be faithful and true,
Let others see Jesus in you.[1]

[1] "Let Others See Jesus in You," by B. B. McKinney. Copyright, 1924, by Robert H. Coleman, and used by permission.

VII

THE SHEPHERD PSALM

PSALM 23

The Lord is my shepherd; I shall not want. He makes me to lie down in green pastures; he leads me beside the still waters. He restores my soul; he leads me in the paths of righteousness for his name's sake. Yea, though I walk through the valley of the shadow of death, I will fear no evil; for thou art with me; thy rod and thy staff they comfort me. Thou preparest a table for me in the presence of mine enemies; thou anointest my head with oil; my cup runs over. Surely goodness and mercy shall follow me all the days of my life, and I will dwell in the house of the Lord forever.

THIS is indeed the pearl of the Psalms, a nightingale singing in the world's night of loneliness and need. It has sung itself into millions of weary hearts and carried into the recesses of these hearts a trust and a confidence akin to that in the heart of the shepherd on Bethlehem's hills. From the throat of the sweet singer comes forth notes of satisfaction, peace, trust, rest, joy, guidance, and fellowship. Language could not be more simple, more chaste, more realistic, or more penetrating. It pictures God, in love with His people, with rest in His bosom, with grace for all our needs, with comfort and joy in sorrow, with a message of hope so sweet and clear that the music breaks forth from the soul.

Through the centuries, it has caught the imagination of children, challenged the thinking of strong young men, proved powerful in midyears of struggle, charmed men and women of advancing years with a new confidence and an undying hope in the continued mercies of God. More griefs have been put to rest by its sweet assurances, more sadness has been driven away, more confidence has been instilled, than tongue can tell or pen record. To know it is to love it. To believe in it is to live a life of victory, a life of joy and peace. To be swept by it, one will find his life triumphant in prayer, in faith, in wholehearted service. Its poetry and its piety are equal, its sweetness and its spirituality unsurpassed.

It was my privilege to conduct the funeral of a young physician in Los Angeles who had literally given his life to save the life of another boy on a steep mountain climb. This brilliant young scientist, who had already made a name for himself in the field of medicine, had written in his well-worn Bible a note naming this psalm as his favorite bit of Scripture. It had a message for him. When we know the full meaning of these six verses, we shall not wonder that a clean young Christian claimed them as his first choice. On the other side of the world, a lieutenant commander was killed instantly by a bomb dropped on the great ship on which he was performing a surgical operation to save the life of a young seaman. He had just written a letter to his mother telling her of his love for, and his joy in, this same good psalm. It meant much to him that day as the chaplain read its heartening words to the men on board. In the midst of war and suffering and death this sacred poem brought courage and solace and renewed hope to men who were going out to die. Its message to human hearts is unbelievably powerful. May we do our best to understand its meaning, and then let it do for us all that the Holy Spirit would work in us.

The author knows the needs of the sheep and the love and thoughtfulness and the care of the shepherd. Weak, foolish, thoughtless, unprotected sheep certainly need a shepherd who will be a provider, preserver, guide, physician, and friend. David, in old age, thought on these attributes of sheep and shepherd and gave to the world this immortal classic. He dared to reach out and call God his very own. *The Lord is my Shepherd.* What a volume of rich content is wrapped in that little pronoun! He is *my* Shepherd! He had an understanding of the nature of God that was far in advance of his day. His personal grip on God was made possible because his God was a loving, personal Father and Friend who could be described as "my Shepherd."

We may divide the psalm into two parts with three verses each or into three parts with two verses each. It can be:

1–3 The Shepherd and the Sheep
4–6 The Host and the Guest
or
1, 2 The Shepherd and the Sheep
3, 4 The Guide and the Traveler
5, 6 The Host and the Guest

We must come around to the realization that God is tremendously concerned about His own individual creature, and that He will not fail to manifest His personal care in life, in death, and beyond the grave. The first line really gives us the key to the whole psalm. Verses two to six tell us what the Shepherd does. They amplify the rich treasures that are mine as a result of the fact that He is my Shepherd. Since I have Him, no want can be beyond the sphere of possibility. He will, by virtue of His office as my Shepherd, provide all the needs, both material and spiritual, that I can possibly have. Because He loves me as the good Shepherd, I shall never want for rest, refreshment, nourishment, forgiveness, restoration, fellowship, guidance, deliverance from fear, comfort in sorrow, victory over enemies, security in troublous hours, joy in the Lord, power for service, or a home at the end of the earthly journey. Does He leave out anything in the world that a soul can possibly need? Every material and every spiritual need is provided for helpless, needy creatures who look to the Shepherd for such satisfactions. Only in Him can they be found. He finds peculiar joy in being the Shepherd because He expresses His inner nature in doing just these things for His own sheep.

He Leads Me Into Rest and Refreshment

He supplies my material needs. The bread of life, the water of life, the rest, the refreshment, the quiet repose in protected surroundings, with the eye of the Shepherd watching over me, all these are mine at the hand of the Good Shepherd. The body, the mind, the soul must be refreshed and prepared for the struggles of the road. He cleanses, heals, encourages, forgives, restores, and revives all the areas of the being. It is His delight to make us over in these hours of quiet retreat. Muscles are relaxed, the strain is taken off, quiet repose comes as a soothing remedy, the heart loses its fear of danger while the sheep rests quietly in the care of the thoughtful Shepherd. This picture is one that brings joy to the heart of all mankind. No one of us could stand the strain of going against the stiff grind without a bit of rest. It is so good of the Shepherd to realize that we need this gracious ministry to fit us for the rough going that is ahead. Our lads in the military circles were pulled back after the hours of hard going to a quieter, safer place for relaxation, restoration, renewing, and recreating. How the weary, tense, discouraged, wrought-up boy was blessed by such kind provision! How we who follow our Shepherd appreciate the green pastures and still waters of refreshment and rest and reviving! Thank God for One who *knoweth our frame, who remembereth that we are dust.* He is our Good Shepherd. He wisely and mercifully restores our souls.

HE LEADS US INTO STRENUOUS ACTIVITIES ON THE OPEN ROAD

The psalmist does not consider the rest and refreshment and relaxation as ends in themselves but interprets them as evidences of a wise leader who seeks to renew the energies so that strenuous activities may be endured. David says that God renews him that He may lead him into the hard work of the everyday grind. A very necessary part of the Christian's life consists in arduous struggle. Duties are to be accepted, burdens are to be borne, foes are to be met, battles are to be fought, hard plodding is in store for us. How will we stand up under the struggles of the road? It will be comforting to know that the same gracious hand that led us into vales of quiet refreshment now leads the way into paths of His own choosing. We shall not want for guidance. We can know we are in right paths if we follow the divine Leader and Guide.

Are you sure that you are in step with Him? Are you responsive to His call to service? Does He have difficulty pulling you away from the quiet, peaceful spot where the green pastures and still waters beckon? What a blessed privilege is ours! *He leads!* The eternal God of all the universe is sufficiently interested in the poorest of us to come as a personal guide to lead us through dangers, snares, hills, valleys, to the victories He has in store for us. It is in these trying experiences that one comes to appreciate the nearness, the wisdom, the friendliness, and the purpose of God. He has been kind and thoughtful and gracious in providing the rest and repose. He is now leading step by step into the rough, rugged, steep hills of danger and difficulty and conflict. He daily demonstrates His purpose for us in the tasks to which He sets our hands. He honors us by subjecting us to hard duties so that His work may be accomplished and so that we may be developed as His people. Is your way hard? Are the burdens heavy and the struggles breath-taking? Maybe it will help you to realize that the Shepherd hopes to make you a better Christian through these adversities.

He Leads Us into and Through Vales of Shadow and Sorrow

Just as the shepherd did not leave his sheep by quiet, still waters but guided them out into the highway for actual struggle, he would occasionally lead them through dangerous mountain defiles where perils of every kind were present. A good leader of sheep would not hesitate to choose one of these narrow defiles as a necessary road to the sunlit meadows on the other side. Enemies might be lurking in hidden places, and dangerous mountain passes might cause fear and wounds. The darkness and gloom of the narrow gorges would set fears going at a rapid rate. The shepherd was there, however, and fears only drove the sheep more closely to him. They became more obedient and devoted as they became more dependent and more frightened.

David, in thinking of those experiences when he had led his sheep through such places, came to appreciate God's goodness and thoughtfulness and faithfulness as the Shepherd of human beings. He says: *Yea, though I walk through the valley of the shadow of death, I will fear no evil for thou art with me.* The word *salmaweth* translated "shadow of death," means literally "deep shadow." He is not thinking of the hour of death down the road after a long life of rich blessings. He is picturing the experiences along the way when sorrow and distress and pain and anguish of soul make the heart break under its heavy load. The good Shepherd knows and understands. He, as a faithful Shepherd, must lead through those harrowing experiences. Some suffering must come. Some days the sun will refuse to shine. Sorrow must have its place in all our lives. Then a great number of these perilous moments and these hours of grief are brought on by my own willful conduct. Those who walk the way with me add their bit of woe to a way that already has enough. Their folly and willfulness coupled with my carelessness and rebellious deeds make many dark valleys for my pilgrim way. Disease, disappointment, sorrow, and the active opposition of Satan bring upon my way far too many of these dark valleys. As a frail human creature, I cannot hope to bear them alone.

My plans were made, I thought my path all bright and clear,
My heart with song o'erflowed, the world seemed full of cheer.
My Lord I wished to serve, to take Him for my guide;
To keep so close that I could feel Him by my side.
           And so I traveled on.

But suddenly, in skies so clear and full of light,
The clouds fell thick and fast, the days seemed changed to night;
Instead of paths so clear and full of things so sweet,
Rough things and thorns and stones seemed all about my feet;
           I scarce could travel on.

I bowed my head and wondered why this change should come,
And murmured—"Lord, is this because of aught I've done?
Has not the path been full enough of pain and care?
Why should not my path again be changed from dark to fair?"
           But I still traveled on.

I listened—quiet and still, there came a voice—
"This path is mine, not thine, I made the choice;
Dear child, this service will be best for thee and me,
If thou wilt simply trust, and leave the end to me."
           And so we traveled on.

How may I count on strength enough to endure to the end? When the heart is breaking, when dark shadows gather, when the sun refuses to shine, when tears flow as a torrent, when all seems dark about me, what am I to do? David, who had experienced more than his normal share of sorrows, tells us the answer. He says: *I will fear no evil for thou art with me.*

He knows that as he meets all these dangers and sorrows and fears he has his divine Shepherd close by his side. *Thou art with me*. Why should I fear when He is near? He walks before me. He knows the way. He knows all the pitfalls and the dangers and the hidden enemies. He knows my own weak frame. Why should I fear when the eternal Creator of everything is by my side. Does the little baby girl fear the fury of the storm at sea when she is securely held by a loving mother? Does the boy fear at night when he can reach over and hold the hand of his big father who sleeps by his side? My Shepherd loves me enough to hold me and protect me and lead me safely through the dark valley into the sunny fields on the other side. Without bitter complaint and ugly self-pity, I will lay my trembling hand in the hand of my Shepherd and move on out into the vales of pain or sorrow, knowing that I am being kept by His power and that through it all He will hold me fast. My Shepherd loves me enough to make possible Calvary with all its suffering and agony and death.

What shall we say about the hour of death? Is that experience included in this verse? Certainly in that hour, as in all the other experiences of the way, He is with us. He fills the dark hours of pain or suffering with light and drives fear away by laying His loving arms about us and leading us out through the tunnel into the land of endless day. But there is no dark valley at death for the Christian. Our Saviour has conquered death, and He comes to welcome us into the glory land beyond the shore. He came back to visit John on the Isle of Patmos and said to him: *Fear not; I am the first and the last. I am he that liveth and was dead; and behold, I am alive for evermore, and have the keys of death and Hades*. He is saying, "Don't be afraid of life, for I have lived. Don't be afraid of death, for I have died. Don't be afraid of eternity, for I hold in my hand the keys to all those mansions over there." Surely we will not be afraid of all life's toil and sorrow and hard places for they are made heavenly places by the presence of this Guide who has proved Himself a loving Friend in all the experiences of the way.

He Leads into a Beautiful Home
at the end of the Journey

The psalmist pictures God as a gracious host who prepares a table for him in the very midst of his enemies. Instead of fear and cringing, there is quiet and order because the Shepherd is there to prepare the delightful banquet and to protect His guest while he enjoys the meal in peace. He exclaims with gratitude: *Surely goodness and mercy shall follow me all the days of my life, and I will dwell in the house of the Lord forever.* Life may be made up of dangers and hard struggles, but he is to be pursued continually by these two divinely given attendants, *goodness and mercy.* What a life it is, to be so carefully tended, so bountifully fed, so securely guarded, so graciously guided, and so tenderly supported by a loving Shepherd! It is most thrilling though when David breaks through with the announcement that a heavenly home awaits us when the toils of this life are ended. The Shepherd graciously invites the weary pilgrim to come in after the toil and stress of the day have been finished. A little girl in telling the story of Enoch's walk with God said, "The man walked and walked and walked and when it became dark God said, 'Enoch, you are nearer my home than yours so you should come in with me,' and he did." Surely in our day we can look forward to that realization since the certainty of a heavenly home has been established by the words of Jesus Himself. When He was ready to leave this earth to go back to be with the Father, He reassured His disciples with the definite promise of the home of the soul. *I go to prepare a place for you. And if I go and prepare a place for you, I will come again and receive you unto myself that where I am there ye may be also.* In this promise, we have an echo of David's early hope. Jesus wants us to be certain of His plans for His own redeemed children. When the hour comes for us to leave this earth, we may be sure that His hand will be in our hand, and that we shall walk the way with Him on the other shore.

This psalm has much in it that is rich and helpful to Christians who think seriously of the kind of preparation for the other world which Jesus emphasized. In the midst of toil and hard work, in the midst of suffering and pain, in the midst of sorrow and distress, we have the abiding presence of the Man of Galilee who *loves us and loosed us from our sins,* and who *has made us a kingdom, priests unto God.* Surely the sorrows and the dangers will be lighted and transformed by the presence of Him who walks by our side.

Dr. John McNeil tells a story of his boyhood days in Glasgow, Scotland. He says that he used to leave the store late at night to make his way across a rough section in which was a deep ravine. Robbers and dangerous men hid themselves in this spot to seize defenseless people and take their money. He says that one particular evening, he was scared almost out of his wits as he made this dangerous journey alone. Suddenly he became conscious of someone walking along the narrow path. He backed up against the overhanging rock and flattened himself out as thin as possible, hoping that the man might pass without recognizing his presence. His little heart was pounding at his throat when suddenly he heard the voice shout, "John! John!" Without a moment's hesitation, he threw himself forward and wrapped his little arms around the knees of the man who had called. It was his father! Joy filled his little heart as fear fled. No one could harm him now. The two walked together along the narrow path toward the humble home. Instead of fear and trembling and panic his heart was bubbling over with joy and confidence. Surely he understood what David meant when he said: *Yea, though I walk through the valley of the shadow of death, I will fear no evil, for thou art with me.*

How can these things be? It all seems so wonderful and attractive that we find ourselves longing for the secret. How can we hope to have such victories? It is all made possible because of the love of God for us and the sacrifice of Jesus Christ who paid it all that we might be ransomed. He died in our place. We received eternal life through faith in Him as our crucified and risen Saviour. The condition of our salvation is faith in Him. The real ground of our redemption is the blood of Christ. He died and rose again for us. Now He lives in us. God the Father is the source of our salvation. God the Son is the channel through which it comes to us. God the Holy Spirit is the agent who makes it effective in us. His provision for us is the costliest transaction ever conceived in the heart of God. It took the precious blood of His own Son to pay the debt. We enter into the full realization of this salvation by complete surrender to Him with the certain trust in Him to provide all our wants. He, as our Shepherd, will guide us and meet all our needs, material and spiritual. We can continue in Him only as the Shepherd continues constantly with us. He helps us bear each burden, strengthens us to meet each temptation, fortifies us to drive out every fear, undergirds us to endure every affliction and sorrow, and prepares us in heart and mind to go joyously into the other land where joys immortal dwell.

Can you say, *the Lord is my Shepherd*? In all of the uncertainty and chaos of this meaningful hour do you dare go out into the unknown without the presence of the eternal Shepherd? Did you meet Him and fall in love with Him in the days of your youth? Have you proved willful and rebellious and have you turned away from the leadership of the holy Shepherd? What a pity! Nothing more tragic could happen to you. What about your home? Was it a place where the

Bible was read and prayer was made and obedient following
was the order of the day? How about it today? Do your children know and love and follow the Shepherd? Life is not
worth living without Him. Your home is not a home in the
full sense if He is not there to bless, to restore, to forgive, to
guide, to sustain, to lead you through the vales of sorrow
into the sunlit hills on the other side and finally into the
Father's presence where a home awaits you. Unless He is
your Shepherd you can never know the unspeakable joys that
you have a right to enjoy as you journey along the way. Why
should you forfeit your right to them? Why blunder and
stumble along when the good Shepherd wants to be your
guide? Can you say with the poet:

> So I go on not knowing,
> I would not if I might;
> I'd rather walk with God in the dark
> Than to walk alone in the light:
> I had rather walk with Him by faith
> Than to walk alone by sight.

My prayer for you is that you may lay your trembling hand
in His own pierced hand and let Him be your Saviour. He
says, *I am come that you may have life and that you may
have it more abundantly*. Eternity alone will reveal all the
full joys that await you as He leads.

VIII

TASTE AND SEE

PSALM 34

I will bless the Lord at all times; his praise shall continually be in my mouth. My soul shall make her boast in the Lord; the humble shall hear and be glad. O magnify the Lord with me, and let us exalt his name together. I sought the Lord, and he heard me, and delivered me from all my fears. They looked unto him, and were radiant; and their faces were not ashamed. This poor man cried, and the Lord heard him, and saved him out of all his troubles. The angel of the Lord encamps round about them that fear him, and delivers them. O taste and see that the Lord is good. Blessed is the man that trusts in him. . . . The Lord is nigh to them that are of a broken heart; and saves such as be of a contrite spirit.

Do you pride yourself on being scientific in your approach to truth? Are you willing to apply the scientific test to three or four of the most practical matters in all the realm of religious thinking? Will you agree to put a very vital matter to the test? Follow with us in an attempt to understand the message of this psalm and you will be delighted with the method he uses in arriving at his powerful convictions.

The psalm is made up of twenty-two verses, each beginning with a separate letter of the Hebrew alphabet except that *Waw* is omitted and *Pe* occurs twice. The first ten verses are devotional in nature and the closing verses are doctrinal or didactic. We shall use only the first division in this study. Without going into the arguments pro and con we are accepting the Davidic authorship and the superscription which tells us of David's experience with the king of Gath and his retirement to the cave of Adullam.

A Vow of Praise (1, 2)

Some signal deliverance has set the joybells ringing in his soul and David declares that he will spend the rest of his days praising the Lord, his Deliverer. How could a man make such a promise? How could he hope to keep it? Surely he has some duties. He is very definite in his determination to sound forth praises to his Saviour who has blessed him. Nothing will stop him from telling others what marvelous things the Lord has done. Paul said: *Rejoice in the Lord always, and again I say rejoice.* The psalmist was willing to let the whole tenor of his life continually repeat to the world his debt to his Redeemer. He has just been delivered from some dangerous experience. He is even now surrounded by those who will take his life. As the head of an outlaw gang, just a step and a half ahead of Saul's men, he can expect plenty of trouble along the way but he dedicates his whole being to the one task of praising and thanking God. Our hats are off to him as he dedicates himself to such a worthy task. Our spirits would be sweeter and more like His if we could give ourselves to praise and thanksgiving. One is at his best when he is praising God. It does something to him. It works wonders in the spirits of others as they look upon one so completely given over to praising God. The music in his soul sets up a beautiful radiance that speaks its message of hope and cheer.

OTHERS INVITED TO JOIN HIM (3)

So far we have had a solo of praise. It has been beautiful to listen to the sweet soloist. So intense is his joy that he feels a genuine hunger to have others join him in his earnest efforts to *magnify the Lord and to exalt His name.* He hopes that his neighbors and friends have within their own minds and hearts reasons for praise and so he begs them to add their voices alongside his in an attempt to render worthy thanksgiving. Together they may produce the kind of shout that will reach the very portals of God's throne room. They may help him *magnify* that holy name by acknowledging and celebrating His supreme greatness. Men should know how great He is. They will *exalt His name* when before the people they confess Him as the one supreme Ruler above all.

> All hail the power of Jesus' name!
> Let angels prostrate fall;
> Bring forth the royal diadem,
> And crown Him Lord of all!

The symphony of praise will delight the heart of God. Neighbors and strangers and aliens will hear and be moved and will bow to worship Him. The poet is calling to you and to me to become members of that enthusiastic choir. We have been redeemed. We know the joys of salvation. We know what He can do for men. How can we refuse to join with other joyous souls in singing praises to our Saviour and Lord?

A PERSONAL EXPERIENCE (4)

The psalmist is always ready to tell of an hour in his own life when God came along to bring joy and deliverance. Many times we find a most interesting account of God's loving intervention when hope was nearly gone. A sincere soul that willingly testifies to the Lord's deliverance can always count on interested listeners. Why should a speaker feel that he should apologize when he relates the story of his own personal touch with God? Through the years men have been blessed by the experience meeting. The word of personal testimony is powerful. In verse four the psalmist bares his soul and reveals something of the depths to which he had fallen, his helpless condition, his misery, his fervent prayer, his earnest search for God, and the instant response of One who snatched him from fear and danger and despair. In his darkest hour he cried out to God in faith, thrust forth his trembling hand into the darkness and found that hand gripped by the strong hand of God. What a glorious sensation! God was there. He was ready and waiting for the feeble call for help. He had full deliverance immediately. From the pit and the miry clay he was lifted to the solid rock. From fog and cloud and darkness he was brought into the marvelous light streaming from God's presence. *Underneath* were *the everlasting arms.* He had an anchor now. He was safe in the keeping of the eternal God. Fears could not live in an atmosphere like that and shouts of praise soon echoed through the air. His heart rejoiced in his new assurance. He had a new faith born of a vital experience with his Redeemer. The new song in his heart brought hope and courage and guidance to others who were seeking the way home.

THE TESTIMONY OF FRIENDS (5, 6)

David has not been content to enjoy God's blessings alone. He has shared his secret with friends. He has not only revealed to them what God has done for him but has induced them to try the same source of rich gifts. Would that we were as conscious of the rich blessings that have come to us because of the love of a Father God. Our own souls have been enriched and our lives have been strangely brightened because of the coming of His Spirit within. The remedy has worked wonders with us. The bells are ringing in our hearts. Let us pray that we may be as willing to help bring these same rich blessings to our neighbors and friends. We may take verses four and six together as referring to the psalmist and verses five and seven as referring to his friends, or we may think of verse six as singling out one of the friends as an example. Perhaps the latter course will be better. In verse six he tells us of a friend who was bowed down under a load of trouble. It was more than he could bear. His grief was too great for articulate prayer but from the deep he cried unto the Lord and instantly the answer came. *He saved him out of all his troubles.* His most beautiful figure is the one that describes for us the downcast faces of certain of his friends who were suffering under some heavy grief or burden. Their faces told the sad story (as faces have a way of doing). He says when *they looked to Him they became radiant.* What a transformation! What a glorious result! Why not try it? How many faces need changing! How many hearts need lifting! Radiant faces are beautiful. (Another reading would translate the first verb as an imperative, making it read: *Look unto Him and be radiant.*) Faces turned to look upon Him must be radiant. We can all appreciate the need for the application of this verse to our own hearts and lives. Radiant faces are sorely needed in this old gloomy world. Christ in the heart makes the difference,

> Turn your eyes upon Jesus
> Look full into His wonderful face
> And the things of earth will grow strangely dim
> In the light of His glory and grace.

Paul tells us (II Corinthians 3:18) how looking upon Him will not only bring radiance but we shall be gradually changed *into the same image.* What a sublime thought! Why not try it? Do you remember when your mother used to take her Bible and go away all alone and spend time with the Lord?

Have you forgotten the radiance and glory in her face as she came back from her secret place with the Lord? The day was different. The load was lighter. The family knew and appreciated the new light in her face and the new richness in her inner soul. Have you become too busy and have you forgotten the secret of the serene heart that comes only to one who takes time out to look unto Him? Do you long for that inner richness that will give you a clear radiance? God is still available.

THE ANGEL ENCAMPS (7)

David was in imminent danger. In the darkness of the wilderness he could imagine a number of Saul's men ready for the attack. They might strike any moment. How could he withstand them? What was his defense? Night after night he must have thought on the perils of his position. Chilling fears gripped him. Out of the history of his people the answer came. Abraham and Jacob and Joshua had known of the presence of a mysterious person known as the *Angel of the Lord* or the *Angel of His Presence*. (Cf. also Joshua 5:14; Zechariah 9:8.) He is Jehovah's special representative in dealing with men. When Abraham had the knife ready to slay his son the holy messenger reversed the divine decree and said: *Thou hast not withheld thy son from me.* To Jacob he said: *I am the God of Bethel.* Later he called the name of the lonely place *Mahanaim,* "two camps." What did he mean by that name? David interprets it to mean that alongside his feeble little camp there is another. He says: *The Angel of the Lord encamps round about them that fear Him and delivereth them.* His little camp was poorly garrisoned and the enemy might easily break through his human guard, but outside that ring is another guard through which any intruder must break before he can get at him. It is a thrilling thought!

When Jesus came, in the fullness of time, to assume His

rightful place as the true *Angel of Jehovah* he took peculiar delight in saying to His disciples, *Lo, I am with you always.* The presence of the Saviour made fears out of place. His power, his love, his willingness to guard and keep, guaranteed a serenity and a peace that brought victory.

Paul comes along and declares *we are therefore more than conquerors through Him that loved us,* and, in another connection, *I can do all things through Christ who strengthens me.* Peter refers to the glory of being *kept by the power of God.* Why should fear find any resting place in our minds? How can we go on in fear and dread when such golden assurances have been given us. *Mahanaim* is still the name of every spot where a lone follower of God pitches his frail tent. He is never alone. *The Lord of Hosts is with us. The God of Jacob is our refuge.*

Four times David assures himself of deliverance. He has no doubt of it since the *Angel of the Lord* is there. He will have pains and sorrows and trials but the great Keeper will not let him be crushed. Surely in our own day we have a source of hope that David did not understand. We have the eternal salvation that gives us life with our Lord forever. We are garrisoned and guarded all the days of our lives by One who has all power in His hands. Fears have no place in the heart of a Christian. He leads.

The Taste Test (8)

In our introduction we promised you the most approved scientific approach to certainty. In this verse we have it. The psalmist does not ask you to take his word for it although he has gone to great lengths to give both his personal testimony and the witness of his friends who found so much joy and so many rich blessings. He suggests the final test that must eventually convince anyone who will honestly submit to it. He says, *taste and see.* You want to be radiant, happy, serene, a conqueror? You are asking how? He merely says, "taste what God has to offer." "Put Him to the test." "Let Him demonstrate His saving and keeping power." Does He hear and answer prayer? Try Him and see. Will He help you get the victory over the tempter? Try Him and see. Will He help you in the hour when your heart is breaking under the weight of a great sorrow? *Taste and see.* Let Him prove it. Paul says: *My God shall supply every need of yours according to the riches in glory by Christ Jesus.* We can agree with David in his word, *Happy is the man who takes refuge in Him.* If we seek He will be found and will help. If we look to Him He will make radiant. If we cry unto Him He will save. If we fear, He will surround with mercies. Even the young lions will be lean and hungry and unsatisfied but God's children will find a marvelous satisfaction in Him that transcends any spoken desire. They have the continuing presence of the eternal *Angel of the Lord* who knows and loves and protects and provides every good thing. *The Lord is my Shepherd, I shall not want.*

APPLICATION

What a blessed lift this psalm gives to the Christian. For sheer beauty and charm it has few equals. It tells of the unceasing goodness of Jehovah. Note the things it says of Him. *He answered me. He delivered me from all my fears. He heard. . . . He saved. His eyes are toward the righteous. . . . His ears are open. Jehovah is nigh. . . . He delivereth. He keepeth. He redeemeth.* In the music of this lovely song we are told of the nearness, the sensitiveness, the power, the ready help, the eternal watchfulness of our God. The author wants others to know, to consider, to hear, to praise, to test, and to enjoy the sacred blessings prepared for those who love Him. He has a marvelous secret that others must have. How can we help others with it?

(1) We need to take literally the emphasis on perpetual thanksgiving and praise. How else can we live since we have come to know and enjoy His gifts? (2) We can recognize the telling value of the old "experience meeting" when individuals who have received rich blessings tell of God's mercy and grace. *Let the redeemed of the Lord say so.* (3) We need to call attention to the beauty of Christian radiance and help lead our friends to the source for a bountiful supply that will transform their faces into radiant pictures of joy and happiness. How beautiful is a radiant face! How effective is the witness when the soul shines forth through heaven-touched eyes! (4) We may make it clear to men that the way to the understanding of spiritual truths is by way of personal experience. Each one must come to his God in individual approach. Only as we discover the realm of spiritual realities for ourselves will we be able to enjoy God's rich treasures. (5) We can assure men of the divinely-given remedy for fear. It is only as a man recognizes the presence of God in his own life that he is able to banish fear. The psalmist was beset by many fears. These fears were doing plenty to wreck his life but he found full deliverance as he came to feel the presence of his God. *Lo, I am with you always* is still the one compelling antidote for fear. (6) We may find a new interest in others and follow the example of the psalmist in leading them to bring all their burdens and fears and sins to the Lord. How many, many souls grope in uncertainty and fear and useless wandering who could be found and brought to the Lord of Life!

We have the greatest opportunity of our lives in making clear to men who do not know the way home that our Saviour is *the way, the truth, the life* and that the way to certainty and peace is to *taste and see.* Only as one is willing to turn to Him and put Him to the test will he ever be in possession of the eternal treasures. Oh that men would *taste and see!* They will if we can present to them radiant faces, glowing hearts, clear faith and a convincing challenge to *taste and see*. It is God's way to victory. It can bring certainty, hope, radiance, the ringing of joybells, a clear assurance, an eternal salvation. Jesus said: *No man cometh to the Father but by me. Him that cometh to me I will in no wise cast out. No man can pluck them out of my Father's hand. He that believeth in me shall never die.*

> Come, every soul by sin oppressed,
> There's mercy with the Lord,
> And He will surely give you rest
> By trusting in his Word.

IX

GRATITUDE

PSALM 103

Bless the Lord, O my soul; and all that is within me, bless his holy name. Bless the Lord, O my soul, and forget not all his benefits. Who forgiveth all thine iniquities; who healeth all thy diseases; who redeemeth thy life from destruction; who crowneth thee with loving-kindness and tender mercies; who satisfieth thy mouth with good things; so that thy youth is renewed like the eagle's. . . . The Lord is merciful and gracious, slow to anger, and plenteous in mercy. He will not always chide; neither will he keep his anger forever. He hath not dealt with us after our sins; nor rewarded us according to our iniquities. For as the heaven is high above the earth, so great is his mercy toward them that fear him. As far as the east is from the west, so far hath he removed our transgressions from us. Like as a father pitieth his children, so the Lord pitieth them that fear him. For he knoweth our frame; he remembereth that we are dust. . . . But the mercy of the Lord is from everlasting to everlasting upon them that fear him, and his righteousness unto children's children. . . . Bless the Lord, ye his angels, that excel in strength, that do his commandments, hearkening unto the voice of his word.

D o you remember the wise saying of the old Negro who, when asked why he so often talked to himself, replied: "Well, sir, you see it's this way. I like to talk to an intelligent person and I like to hear an intelligent person talk." The author of this psalm calls his own soul in and exerts his powers in stirring up gratitude. He realizes that the garden of his heart grows many flowers but the rare flower, called gratitude, is not being cultivated in that garden. He wants something done about it. He is conscious of the close kinship that exists between the word "think" and the word "thank." He wants to set his mind on the gifts and mercies of God so that this priceless flower will grow. He seeks to stir his own soul to praise and thanksgiving. Do we have a greater need today? How about your garden? Do we accept God's mercies and use them without turning our hearts to the Giver of all these blessings?

Few psalms have found their way into the hearts of men so completely as this favorite of the favorites. No psalm is more beautiful. Its remarkable tenderness, its childlike trustfulness, its buoyant hopefulness, anticipate the spirit of the New Testament. No cloud appears on the horizon, no jarring note sounds, no word of complaint is heard, no note of sadness in the music comes to weaken the glad recital of praise. No purer outburst of praise and gratitude can be found in all the Scriptures. Untouched as it is by sorrow and complaint it becomes a matchless prescription for those who mourn and for those who have lost hope.

The psalmist is a remarkable man. His purity of heart and thought is apparent in every line. His deep humility in the presence of God and God's mercies reveals to us depths that attract us. His keen sense of sin fitted him to see and understand the heart of God and to appeal to other human beings to submit to the moral surgery that alone can give life and joy and peace. His knowledge of, and respect for, God's revelation to men is outstanding. That has led him to understand some of the deeper mysteries of God's grace. His depth of insight and his breadth of affection at once stamp him as an interpreter of God's will to men. His grasp of the central theme of the New Testament and his simple presentation of the fact that *God is love* will always keep us in debt to him. He knew God and this intimate knowledge made it possible for these great truths to be presented. Thank God for the psalmist and for his message to us.

In verses one through five he has a talk with his own soul and gratefully records God's individual gifts to him. In verses six through ten he gives vivid illustrations of God's goodness to Israel. Verses eleven through fourteen tell of God's love that makes him a forgiving God. In verses fifteen through eighteen the contrast between man's brief sojourn on earth and the eternity of God's mercy is pictured. Verses nineteen through twenty-two call upon the whole universe to praise the name of the One who so clearly deserves universal gratitude.

Bless the Lord (1, 2)

It is interesting to see the great theologian call his own soul on the carpet and set forth a serious lack in the thinking and in the behavior of the individual. Do we ever check up on ourselves and frankly make note of the presence of certain ugly failures in our inner being? Try it. It will help. The psalmist finds that gratitude is missing. What a tragedy! Read his prescription in verse one and ponder over the effect of that remedy if faithfully taken. What cures could be effected by that simple prescription! How we need that powerful word today! *Bless the Lord, O my soul: and all that is within me, bless His holy name.* He summons all his faculties and the powers of his whole being to unite in gratitude and praise of Jehovah. Why should we wait for a day in November to express the deep sense of gratitude? Perhaps the psalmist should get hold of our minds and call us back to something of this same emphasis.

COUNTING HIS BLESSINGS (3-5)

In calling on his soul to pour forth thanksgiving the author speaks of four "alls": *all* our faculties, *all* his mercies, *all* our iniquities, *all* our diseases. With these in mind he begins to recount the marvelous benefits God has showered upon him. He is keeping always in the forefront of his mind the consciousness of sin and man's need for cleansing and forgiveness. In naming the blessings he begins with forgiveness and ends with the gift of immortal youth. He is not unmindful of the revelation God has made through Moses and the prophets and through the avenue of his own experience. What a storehouse of knowledge has come by inspiration! He knows much of the divine nature, the divine will, the divinely projected program for the salvation of the souls of men. How grateful he is for the clear picture he has of his God! He knows of Him as a Father who loves, protects, guides, and forgives His own children.

The six things he does for his creatures are: *forgives, heals, redeems, crowns, satisfies, renews*. Any of these is sufficient for a whole lifetime of praise. Each of them calls forth our best. When they are put together in such rapid succession they almost take our breath away. Just as in Psalm 32 we find a sense of God's way of dealing with sin. Full forgiveness is the only way. He forgives because He loves. He applies an overflowing supply of that plenteous grace that wipes out the sin and forgives the sinner. Man's supreme need is thus supplied by the Father who works out His eternal purpose in man's salvation to the abundant life. Healing comes as a necessary step following forgiveness. He freely gives peace and solace and the kind of quiet confidence and serenity of soul that makes for full living. How often do we pause to thank Him for health of body and mind? When He has heard our prayer and healed us how can we fail to express gratitude? The poet's life has been literally snatched back from the very jaws of the grave. He finds it in his heart to recognize the divine power and render thanks. Since he is forgiven and healed and given life again he is now fit for the coronation scene (cf. Psalm 8:5). The Father's hand has been stretched out to crown his head with evidences of the divine approval and love.

In the midst of all this he suddenly realizes that his God satisfies. What a boon! Full satisfaction of every desire is almost too much to ask. The psalmist in his joyful recognition of God's blessings is ready to praise him for bringing complete satisfaction. How can such a man grow old! His body may lose some of its youthfulness but his soul is constantly renewed so that perpetual youth is his. Do you know anyone who does not dread old age? Who wants to grow old? All the remedies and prescriptions and fountains of youth will fail to keep the house in which we live from falling apart. We will grow old physically. The psalmist is thanking God that he has eternal springtime in his heart. His divine Lover had provided the elixir that kept his soul eternally young. Do you have that secret formula? Are you using God's prescription? Does He live within your heart? The psalmist calls on you to break forth in praise to God. It is difficult for us to see the full richness included in the words of these opening verses unless we get our minds and hearts in tune and with shouts of thanksgiving bring praise to Him.

ILLUSTRATIONS OF GOD'S GOODNESS (6-10)

When the radiant singer has talked to himself concerning these benefits he is swept with a desire to tell others of his gratitude. *Let the redeemed of the Lord say so* has always been an appropriate word for one who feels a swell of gratitude within his heart. How it would help if all grateful

Christians would express the deep tides of the soul! It would help the one who does the telling. It would gladden the heart of the one to whom he tells it. It would bring great joy to the heart of God. You have heard the story of the tired minister who, in the midst of preparing a sermon, heard the door open and the voice of his little girl say: "Daddy, may I come in?" When asked what she wanted she replied: "I don't want a thing. I just want to put my little arms around your neck and tell you how much I love you." Does anyone want to hazard a guess as to how much good those sweet words did for that worn man of God? Why not cultivate the grace of gratitude while ears that can still hear can be blessed by the glowing words? Would you prefer having your flowers while you can still enjoy them?

In verses six and seven the psalmist refers to the marvelous revelation that God has given of Himself through Moses and the books of the Torah. He thanks because he knows God as one who acts as only God can act. In every emergency and crisis of the world's history the eternal Creator has proved adequate and just and dependable and unbiased. Not once has He behaved in any other way. In no instance has He lacked power or failed to execute His own divine will as right and justice demanded. All through the centuries He is revealed as a bountiful giver of heart-satisfying blessings.

Verses eight and nine continue the description of what he has learned about God. He has found Him to be *full of compassion and gracious, slow to anger and abundant in loving-kindness.* What a beautiful picture of God! Where did he find it? How true still in our day since Christ has come to make even more vivid the colors in this old portrait of God. The righteous anger of God must blaze against sin and every form of unrighteousness, but there are mercy and compassion present in such abundant quantities that the sinner can always know that he is in the hands of one whose heart is full of love. The psalmist is still dealing with his favorite idea of forgiveness. The anger is held back as long as justice can possibly allow and then the punishment is dictated by the great Lover with the divine purpose always at the center of the picture. He keeps His loving-kindness burning as a continuous flame while His anger flashes only at stated intervals when no other remedy is adequate. He will not be continually chiding or nagging or beating like a foolish mother or father who never ceases to find fault. Our sins have been many. His mercy is so great that no one of us has ever received full punishment. In the light of Jesus' teachings we are destined to see evidences of this that will make the psalmist's picture seem elementary. Eternity alone can reveal the fullness of His merciful gifts to us.

God's Forgiving Love (11-14)

It is difficult to find distances great enough to contain his conception of the love of his God. How high is it to the zenith directly above? How far is it from the East to the West? It may be that the modern scientist has been able to measure such distances with accuracy but the psalmist included it all in his metaphors and his beautiful poetry. Scientists tell us of worlds so far away that light coming to the earth from them at the rate of eleven million miles per minute must travel millions and millions of years to reach us. Every inch of that limitless space was wrapped up in our author's lovely picture. He exhausted words and included all space in expressing the towering height of God's mercy and the completeness of His removal of sin from us. To him forgiveness and cleansing are inseparably united. His forgiving love makes both possible.

Are you asking how the psalmist knows all this about God? We are sure he would remind you again of his dependence upon God's revelation for much of it but we may

be sure that even more of this richer and deeper knowledge
has come through experience. Hosea and Jeremiah and
David learned those rich truths about God from close touch
with Him in darkest hours of grief and loneliness and suffering. After all one never really knows God apart from the
teaching in this bitter school. Our author was giving us the
riches he had gathered from firsthand experience. He knew
God.

In verse thirteen he drives in where our hearts can understand. We might not follow him all the way through the
galaxies and star cities of the heavens above, but when he
tells us that he has found God to be a compassionate Father
he gets down where we follow him fully. *Like as a Father
pitieth His children, so the Lord pitieth them that fear Him.*
He has already learned that sublime truth that Jesus emphasized. Jesus would go further and show that earth's grandest
example of father love would be but a blurred copy of the
original and that the great Father's love would transcend
any human manifestation. He tells us of the wayward boy
who spent his substance in the far country not to let us see
a picture of the boy's rebellion and want, but to show us
the sublime picture of the heart of our heavenly Father who
yearned, watched for, and loved him every moment of his
life. This psalm comes nearer showing us the Father than
anything else until Jesus of Nazareth came to give us His
perfect picture of His Father.

Eagerly he goes on, in verse fourteen, to give us another
illustration of God's mercy toward us. He says that the great
Creator knows all of our frailty and brittleness and weakness.
Because man is but a dust-formed bit of fragile crockery he
must be dealt with by a tender hand. A hard blow from the
mighty, crushing hand of the Creator could "break him as
a potter's vessel is broken." Our God, knowing all this frail
structure, handles us tenderly and as love would prompt. It

is an exquisite picture of true fatherly love dealing with a delicately constructed son as only a divine Father can.

God's Mercy Endures (15-18)

For a moment one would think the psalm is going to dip into the sorrowful vein when we are called on to think of the brevity of man's existence, but we soon see that he is concerned primarily with the amazing grace of God that transcends every other consideration. Remembering man's brief existence on this earth turns our thoughts to God's eternal years. Soon we are lost in contemplation of this eternal purpose and the yearnings of His fatherly heart for His own creatures. Men may pass away but Jehovah's covenant faithfulness endures. Upon that solid rock man's faith may find security. Children and grandchildren can be safe in His keeping. It is rather thrilling to know that your grandchildren are to be kept, guarded, loved and forgiven by that same changeless Father who loves with an undying love and whose grace is as boundless as the sea.

Universal Praise Invited (19-22)

The psalmist, recognizing the supreme and universal sovereignty of Jehovah, calls on the whole universe to unite in praising Him. The throne is fully established guaranteeing stability and eternal existence. God is the mighty Ruler of every part of His vast creation. Let angels and ministers and all his works praise and magnify His name together. What a powerful blast of praise will go up from every inch of space, from the throats of all angels, messengers, and human beings! Let angels not only stand at attention ready to do the bidding of the Lord but let them burst forth in unanimous praise and thanksgiving. Let His ministers make the hills and clouds resound with music as no people has ever heard. Let the choir invisible take up the shout of praise until heaven itself will be filled with the purest music ever uttered.

Suddenly from the transcendent heights with shouts of praise from all the heavenly hosts and from every created thing ringing triumphantly, our author swings back to himself and closes, as he began, with an earnest call to his own heart to *bless the Lord*. His heart is almost breaking with joy and gratitude. He had not realized all the depths and heights and breadths of the love of his Father. He will tell of His love and compassion and willingness to forgive sins. What a marvelous challenge to all our hearts! Surely you and I will want to bow humbly at His feet and crown Him Lord of Lords and pour forth every ounce of praise and thanksgiving that our poor frame can give.

> *Bless the Lord, O my soul*
> *And all that is within me, bless His holy name.*

X

THE WORTHY WORSHIPER

PSALM 15

Lord, who shall abide in thy tabernacle? Who shall dwell in thy holy hill? He that walks uprightly, and works righteousness, and speaks truth in his heart. He that backbites not with his tongue, nor does evil to his neighbor, nor takes up a reproach against his neighbor. In whose eyes a reprobate person is abhorred; but he honors them that fear the Lord. He that swears to his own hurt, and changes not. He that puts not out his money to usury, nor takes a bribe against the innocent. He that does these things shall never be moved.

A MAN has a beautiful country estate with every imaginable luxury and delicacy and comfort. He sets out to invite a number of guests to share those blessings with him. Before he settles definitely on the list of guests he must be certain that no one of those invited will mar the fellowship and be out of place among the other invited friends. It would not do to have one in that company who might at any moment upset the life of the group and embarrass the host. It is clear to us that the host has a perfect right to lay down the rules, set up the standards and conduct any examination that might be necessary. He wants to be sure that each person will fit into the picture, enjoy the hospitality and contribute to the higher atmosphere of the place.

The author of our psalm uses this figure and develops for

us the picture of the ideal guest in God's house. Just as in Psalm 23 God is described as the Host and His creatures are thought of as guests in His house. At any rate they are seen as coming to His house for worship or perhaps as walking companions, in the same figure as we saw used of Enoch (*He walked with God*). The Host in His own home sees fit to invite guests to share the hospitality, the delights, the protection, the security, and the blessings that are so bountifully provided.

In holy awe the poet begins to think on the moral and ethical and spiritual requirements that a holy God might require for entrance. We do not wonder at his anxiety when we remember the timidity and fear that used to be in our young hearts when we were left alone with the minister or when we contemplated a visit to the home of a venerable man of God whose very life seemed to have the sanctity of the other shore. What would you do if you were called out from your regular duties to spend a long time in the company of God's saintliest character? How long could you talk on subjects that would interest him? How carefully you would have to guard your thoughts and words and deeds! How much scrubbing you would have to do to give you the sense of being clean enough for his presence! How would you go about getting ready for that visit?

May we pause here to realize the marvelous boon that is ours in being admitted to God's presence both as a humble worshiper and as a chastened walker along with God. Even though we may never be permitted to visit in the palatial homes of the world's great, we do have the invitation to come to His door to find the divine hospitality that will be more precious than words can describe. It is true! We may be God's guests. He wants us to come. He longs to see us approach His holy tent. In Palestine the stranger who took refuge in the tent of the wild Bedouin was safe from all harm. Protection, food, drink, hospitable attention, could be guaranteed. As long as he chose to stay he was welcome to share in all the bountiful provisions of his abode.

In this brief poem of five simple verses the psalmist gives us his idea of the requirements that one must meet before he is an acceptable worshiper of Jehovah and before he may enjoy the rich fellowship with the divine Host. In verse one the question is put. In the second verse the answer is given in general terms. None but the man of integrity, the man of justice, the man of truthfulness can hope to qualify. Nothing is said of forms or ceremonies or ritual or offerings, or robes or postures. No special priestly purification or ritualistic ceremonialism is required. Plainly he is of the opinion that the qualities that fit a man for divine companionship are the great ethical qualities. In verses three to five the psalmist seeks to paint the guest from the outside, giving us instances in his life that demonstrate the nature of his heart and mind. With vividness and frankness he illustrates the way his character has been controlled by these principles. He shows us how he has lived with all types of men in the rough going of life. In this way he claims the real man reveals himself. Habits are described as acts. A picture is taken as he works and lives with men. In the closing line he gives a promise of blessing.

What are the conditions? When God meets you at the door of the tent and holds up his measuring stick or brings out his record of your words and thoughts and deeds or asks you to step before his fluoroscope, what will be required of the prospective guest? Are you ready to submit to the examination? Would you like to know what an Old Testament saint considered the vital qualities of soul? Stated positively, he must be a man of integrity, a man who speaks the truth and a man who is actively engaged in works of righteousness. By walk, by word, by work, he is God's man. Integrity is the rule of his life. The word used to describe his walk is *tamim*. It is a big word in Hebrew. It is usually translated "perfect" but can be rendered "complete," "without blemish," "blameless," "sincere," "whole." It certainly contains the idea of love for, and complete devotion to, God as well as complete integrity as human beings are met. His heart, his attitude, his character, are right as God looks upon him. As he walks before God there are no shady spots, nothing of insincerity or sham or hypocrisy. The devil does not hold sway in his life. Utter honesty controls not only his words but all his dealings. He guards every word lest he say more than he actually intends. He is actively engaged in contributing to the needs of the people around him. God can count on him to be one of His representatives in the community to let the divine grace flow into needy hearts. *Works of righteousness* are sorely needed in our world. It is a rare individual who can qualify fully as God's earthly representative to pass on the grace consigned to others.

Thus we see that the ideal guest walks blamelessly, speaks truthfully, works righteousness. As he *speaks truth* his whole heart goes along with the word. He is sincere and behaves always as one who is conscientious and straight in his attitudes and intentions. What he says and does may not always be the popular thing but he prefers absolute truth and integrity at any cost. Men may always know exactly where he stands on every moral question. No question of profits or personal advancement or popular favor will affect either his walk, his word, or his work. When God looks on and registers His decision concerning **the guest, it** cheers us to know that these qualities are the ones that gain admittance to His throne room. Jesus said: *Blessed are the pure in heart for they shall see God.* Our poet came very near to that New Testament line in his delineation of the ideal guest.

In addition to these positive qualities, described in verse

two, we find certain negative tests that he must face. There are certain things that must not be found in the heart and life and conduct of the ideal worshiper. He set certain refusals as the guiding stars by which he charted his course. These refusals and these victories in the realm of conduct are possible because of the sterling character that has already been pictured.

He refuses to let his tongue get out of control and go off to injure innocent bystanders. How often a host has been embarrassed by such behavior on the part of an invited guest! The psalmist says that God cannot and will not allow such a creature to have access to his circle of friends. He must be willing to guard his tongue. Better still he will not have it in his heart to say hurtful things. After all perhaps we are too hard on the tongue. It is a helpless little being. No word can be spoken by it until the order comes from the brain. It is merely a spoon or ladle that reaches back into the heart and gathers up a bit of whatever is there and throws it forth into the very face or ear of someone who happens to be near. *Keep thy heart with all diligence for out of it are the issues of life.* We do not need to fear this man because he does not *foot it around* telling things that are untrue, to hurt and wound and offend.

He refuses to go out to find some dead rat that might much better remain buried and drag the offensive thing around to embarrass one who is doing his best to make a new beginning with God's help and encouragement. He cannot find it in his heart to pass on something that can do no good. An evil rumor dies without the slightest encouragement. When will we learn how severely God rebukes the slanderer, the talebearer, the defamer, the gossiper? Nothing pleases the devil any more than to have one or two of them in a church to mar the fellowship, offend the pure minds and sensitive souls, disrupt friendships and weaken the impact of the church. When will men and women who claim to be Christians become Christian in that one particular at least? God grant that this paragraph may be used to break the heart of any person who is guilty. God hates it. The devil loves it. The psalmist says you need not worry about this friend of his for he has no intention of doing anything that so grievously offends the great Host. He refuses to become a sewer pipe to carry ugly and unfounded reports. The poet thinks that a person like that is not fit to be in God's lovely assembly. He is not saying that the man is not saved. That is not his subject. He is saying that God will not select him as a fit companion for hours of delightful fellowship.

He is able to read character and understand the hearts of men and has moral courage to evaluate them as they are. He estimates a scoundrel at face value and no extenuating circumstance will make him give undeserved standing to him. He refuses to whitewash iniquity. It takes a lot of courage to measure up there but he has something of the divine hatred for sin. Jesus refused to treat some of his famous contemporaries as they were accustomed to receive attention. Paul was strangely powerful in his straight talk to those who were expecting the usual recognition. This reprobate is one who is not good metal (Jeremiah 6:30) but valueless dross. Our poet treats him with fully merited contempt. It is a part of his honest heart's behavior. All his money and his social standing count for nothing to this man who is such a worthy candidate for Jehovah's tent.

In that same category he looks up to and honors one who is true metal even though he has no money or social prestige. He has special honor for the humble man whom the world tends to ignore. He is keen enough, honest enough, courageous enough and Christlike enough to honor the godly man who so richly deserves honor. It is refreshing to find

such fine discrimination in the field of ethics. This discernment brings joy to the heart of the great Examiner at the
door of the tent.

He keeps his word no matter what the cost. Have you
heard it said of some good man, "His word is as good as his
bond"? Does that statement stir your soul? When a promise
is made it is a sacred thing. No witnesses are necessary. No
contracts or collateral or endorser will be asked. Conditions
and circumstances may change. It may cost a great deal in
material things to keep that promise but there is a sanctity
about it that makes it too sacred to be broken. Throughout
his whole life he has lived by that ideal. He holds to the sacredness of his promise because of that inner honesty of soul that
makes dishonest behavior completely impossible. He has no
struggle over mere instances of conduct because the heart is
full of that which makes automatic the routine decisions of
life. How fervently do we pray that our young men and women
may have built into the very warp and woof of their character
the strands that will prove steadfast in the hours of stress and
strain and storm! God is still looking for those who are endowed with this powerful sense of that which is right and
honorable and sacred. Some of us are found lacking when
God's X-ray picture of our hearts is developed and the true
status is revealed.

He refuses to enrich himself at the expense of an unfortunate neighbor. He is not out to make money. Usury and
bribery are not sins of his. He has no compelling desires for
a lot of money. He much prefers helping a neighbor without
interest than having money come back to him from one who
was in need. In those days men did not borrow money except
in dire necessity. Distress drove them to it. The only person
who lent money dealt with a pitiful soul in distress. This
man utterly refused to take advantage of his neighbor in any
such way. He had a genuine love in his heart for other in-

dividuals and the temptation to break the laws of God to enrich himself had no power over him. It is always wrong to take advantage of another's necessity. Amos thundered against this unholy practice. Jesus drove the lesson home with power.

He refuses to employ money to interfere with the course of justice. Bribery has been a curse to mankind's way for a long time. In the Old Testament day they had no trained judges with adequate salaries to measure out justice to rich and poor alike. The judge was an older man in the community who claimed the right to settle disputes. Since he had no income it was quite a temptation to take bribes from men who had plenty to help win their cases. The poor man in that court had almost no chance to win his case. What is our status today? Can we count on absolute equality for the poor, the ignorant, the minority group? It is not always bribery, but a preponderance of money and legal talent and influential witnesses and the power of the press can go a long way toward thwarting justice and bringing about the same tragic results. Our psalmist represents the ideal worshiper as one whose hands are clean because his heart is devoid of the ugly selfishness that makes for cruelty and injustice and tragedy. The all-seeing eye of God sees the quality of soul that has kept him from behavior that befits the devil rather than one *created in the image of God*. Unfortunately we have far too many who *bite the poor* and take advantage of the unfortunate and condemn the innocent for gain. May God help us to see ourselves as God sees us and pattern our ways according to the leading of hearts that have been cleansed by His own touch.

In the closing line the poet asserts that such a man as he has pictured will not only gain entrance into the presence of God with the divine approval but will be securely anchored and grounded so that no storm will dislodge him from his

God-given place of refuge. It is a great promise to men who dread feeling the solid base of life crumble beneath them. Every man wants security. He loves to feel his anchor hold in the worst storm. He rejoices in the solid rock that will stand always. He finds just that assurance in this last word of the psalm. *He shall not be moved.* His anchor holds. The perfect tranquillity and security of the believer who is a guest in Jehovah's house is an amazing tonic to the trusting soul. He will stand unmoved though all the world about him should be shaken. He is secure and safe in Him. John says: *The world passes away and the lust thereof, but he that doeth the will of God abideth forever.* Jesus said: *No man can pluck them out of my Father's hand.*

> How firm a foundation, ye saints of the Lord,
> Is laid for your faith in His excellent word!
> What more can He say than to you He hath said,
> You who unto Jesus for refuge have fled?
>
> The soul that on Jesus hath leaned for repose,
> I will not, I will not desert to its foes;
> That soul, tho' all hell should endeavor to shake,
> I'll never, no, never, no, never forsake!

How may I attain this? How may I have the inner heart prepared for such an examination? It all seems so impossible and high and unbelievable. Who is sufficient for such things? Christ alone can make it possible. Only as He comes and transforms the heart into a dwelling place of the Holy Spirit can the way be opened for the spirit that will qualify me for the X-ray examination. Each of us wants to be a worthy worshiper. Christ is the answer. He comes and cleanses and restores and re-creates so that we can stand in the door of the tent with clean hands, pure hearts, restored minds and chastened wills. He sets the bells going in our hearts and gives us the power to be *more than conquerors.* He gives victory.

Is it asking too much to urge our young people to examine these exquisite lives and see clearly the high standard set up for one who would please God? When that picture is clear, may they have the courage to look as honestly into their own hearts and see the thoughts, the motives, the attitudes, the tendencies, and go courageously about the task of preparing for His presence? Is it not good to know that we are invited to come into His tent for the intimate fellowship that will prove so precious? Surely we cannot fail to sense the significance of that divinely-given privilege. We will go to any length to make ourselves fit to walk with the King. He has a right to our best. He can make demands. He has high purposes for us. He loves us so much that we cannot disappoint him. He can cleanse and restore and bring joy to all our hearts.

> One thing I of the Lord desire,
> Tho' all my path hath miry been;
> Be it by water or by fire,
> O make me clean!
> O make me clean!

XI

DE PROFUNDIS

PSALM 130

Out of the depths have I cried unto thee, O Lord. Lord, hear my voice. Let thine ears be attentive to the voice of my supplications. If thou, Lord, shouldst mark iniquities, O Lord, who shall stand? But there is forgiveness with thee, that thou mayst be feared. I wait for the Lord, my soul waits; and in his word do I hope. My soul waits for the Lord more than they that watch for the morning. I say, more than they that watch for the morning. Let Israel hope in the Lord; for with the Lord there is mercy, and with him is plenteous redemption.

CAN you imagine a deep, abandoned well in a remote section of the country with no means of escape? Into it has fallen an unfortunate victim who realizes that it is utterly impossible for him to get out and that the probability of being found is exceedingly slim. He is desperate. How can he do anything that will help? His only chance is to cry out with all his might in the hope that someone will hear and come to his rescue. Even though his voice is worn out and his strength exhausted he must continue to call for help.

That is the situation described by our psalmist in the text before us. He has analyzed his situation fully and realizes that his deepest need is for forgiveness and that God alone can handle that matter. No one else can do a thing with sin. It is strangely akin to the opening verses of Psalm 40 and deals with the same great problem as David faced in Psalms 51 and 32. Sin makes the picture a tragic one. The blood of bulls and rams and goats will be utterly useless in effecting his salvation. No human remedy will avail. He must depend upon the mercy of God to provide forgiveness and restoration as well as cleansing.

The psalm is one of the seven penitential psalms and one of the four which Luther called the "Pauline Psalms." Sir Noël Paton has created on canvas a classic picture delineating the deliverance which God works when he hears the penitent cry of a humble soul. He has painted a frail female figure, Psyche, struggling vainly to extricate herself from the bog into which her body has mired. In response to her cry the Saviour comes just in time to snatch the exhausted girl from the mire. Human faith has been met by divine faithfulness and victory is assured. The arms of the limp form of Psyche seem so weak as compared with the powerful arms of the Good Shepherd who lifts her to safety and to life. Faith helps but it is the strong arm of the Saviour who saves her. We feel like pausing to shout: "Hallelujah! What a Saviour!" The redeeming arm of the Lord has snatched a helpless sinner from ruin and death. It is grace that has done it. Divine love in action has won the victory. Because Jesus died on Calvary a way is opened for other repentant suppliants to find the same source of mercy and pardon. His ear is ever listening for the cry of one who recognizes his dire peril and calls out for mercy.

The Prayer of a Piteous Penitent for Pardon (1-4)

In verses one and two we have the urgent cry for help as he feels himself on the very verge of being swallowed up. He has struggled and sought escape only to find himself sucked into the mire a bit deeper with every twist of his body. His only hope is that someone will hear and come to save him. He prays and calls and hopes. Is it not true that any individual must come to that realization before even the Saviour can step in to do His work?

When we turn to the third verse we are faced with a dark fear that clouds his face and chills his very soul. It is as if he hears footsteps and realizes some person is actually coming. He recognizes the Deliverer. His fear comes from the realization that sin has dominion in his life and that God who is holy cannot look upon sin with even the slightest degree of allowance. He is actually afraid of his divine Rescuer. How can he hope to meet the holy God who is at the same time a righteous Judge? He says: *If thou shouldst keep my sins in remembrance* (instead of blotting them out of the record book) *O Lord, who can stand before thee?* It is a sobering thought! How can sinful man with a whole multitude of sins written down against him hope to stand when he is called before the Judge? It is a question that calls for serious thought. Coverdale translated it: *If thou, Lord, wilt be extreme to mark what is done amiss, who shall stand?* The psalmist has sinned against Him as the God of love and now he trembles at the prospect of having to meet him as the God of power. He knows that he is a sinner, that his heart is not true to Jehovah, that he has sinned in breaking the marriage bond. How can he do other than turn to sink down in the mire again? Hope is gone in the light of sin and sin's consequences. How many anxious souls have turned back under the power of this dread realization? Who can stand? Would that sinners today could be profoundly stirred by this alarming truth. The day is coming for all of us when we shall meet Him. How can any man hope to stand in the judgment in the presence of the holy God, the Judge of all men?

Verse four gives the heartening news that God forgives

and all is well. Even the vilest sinner can hope and rejoice for the God who is careful to mark every sin and every error has a heart full of mercy and can forgive. It is the same picture that Hosea presents when he represents God as saying: *How shall I give thee up, Ephraim? How shall I deliver thee, Israel? How shall I make thee as Admah? How shall I set thee as Zeboim? My compassions are kindled together.* Even though punishment was richly deserved the God of love would not insist on utter extermination, for love could always find a way. Just as Hosea made it possible for his wayward wife to be brought back with full forgiveness even so would the eternal Lover provide the price and extend the forgiveness that Israel needed. It is a sublime conception. It calms and reassures the psalmist in his hour of agony. It should be as helpful to us today. We have the added assurance that comes from knowing that our Saviour, God's only begotten Son, has made forgiveness certain through his suffering and death and resurrection. The sin of man may be deep but the forgiveness of God is deeper. Covenant love can and will wipe out the guilt and stain of sin. John Newton knew this sublime truth and recorded something of its riches in his immortal hymn.

> Amazing grace! how sweet the sound,
> That saved a wretch like me!
> I once was lost, but now am found,
> Was blind, but now I see.
>
> 'Twas grace that taught my heart to fear,
> And grace my fears relieved;
> How precious did that grace appear
> The hour I first believed.
>
> Thro' many dangers, toils and snares,
> I have already come;
> 'Tis grace hath bro't me safe thus far,
> And grace will lead me home.

When we've been there ten thousand years,
Bright shining as the sun,
We've no less days to sing God's praise
Than when we first begun.

In Psalms 51 and 32 we are brought face to face with this forgiving love in its fullest expression. Sin had its inning. An accusing conscience did its work. David heard the accusation from the prophet, *Thou art the man!* In sincere penitence he took his confession to God. Nothing was held back; no one else was blamed; no excuses were offered. He understood that the blood of sacrifices could not help at all. Boldly he cast himself on the mercy of a loving God. *I said, I will confess my transgressions unto the Lord: And thou—thou forgavest the iniquity of my sin.* That tells the story in full. In clear, vivid lines the entire transaction is pictured. Forgiveness came to the great sinner when he appealed to the love of God in sincere confession. God's unlimited mercy made victory possible. Full forgiveness is available today to everyone who comes to the Father through His Son, our Saviour. When will we ever learn the remedy and understand the heart of the forgiving Father?

THE FORGIVEN SINNER TRUSTS AND HOPES (5-8)

Forgiveness is not all that the sinner needs. Even though he has received pardon from the hands of God he will still suffer throughout life and will need patience to endure and hope to inspire. He must know that *underneath are the everlasting arms* to undergird and bless. David's sins were forgiven but he was still bowed under suffering and tragedies and heartaches. The little son died, the other sons gave him untold trouble. The consequences of sin continued as long as he lived. His old heart was crushed when the willful Absalom brought disgrace and death upon himself. His sin was forgiven but sorrow and suffering and heartache remained as his portion all the way. He needed a Spirit-taught patience that would provide strength for the tasks and the struggles of life. This psalmist is praying that he may have a deathless hope that holds on in the long hours of the blackest night, always confident of the sunrise. He turned his soul toward Jehovah in childlike trust and in that spirit he found inner strength to watch for the dawn with hope and without fear. His faith in God made him confident even in the storm. He knew God was there. A boy was spending his first night in a tent with his father in the northern woods. In the middle of the night he was awakened by the howling of wolves. When his little hand reached over and rested on his father's shoulder, the father said: "What is it, son? Do you want something?" The boy replied: "No, dad, I just want to know you are there." When we know that He is with us it will be possible to undergo suffering, endure cruel treatment, face darkness and gloom, grapple with the tempter, and wait with a sublime patience through the long night for the coming of the dawn.

Our psalmist is ready to endure any sorrow or pain or disappointment through the long night if he can be reassured by the presence of his God. It is a bit strange too because in verse three he was afraid of this very same God and dreaded His approach. What is the secret? How is it that he now looks for this powerful One, who has plenty of power to crush him, to come to roll back the dark shadows and bring in the glorious morning? He knows Him now as the loving forgiver who will be on his side when He comes. Job catches something of the beauty of this thought when, after doubts and questions have torn his soul, he affirms: *For I know that my Redeemer liveth, and that he shall stand at the latter day upon the earth: And though after my skin worms destroy this body, yet in my flesh shall I see God: Whom I shall see for myself, and mine eyes shall behold, and not another.*

Is that not the very truth which Paul makes clear when he tells us of his experiences with his thorn in the flesh? How earnestly he prayed that the thorn might be removed! Over and over again he begged for his answer. The only reply was: *My grace is sufficient for thee.* In the midst of suffering and irritation and lessened physical powers he must learn to endure, knowing that the supply of grace was plenteous and that under the hurt of divine discipline he was to wait patiently for God's own time to bring sweet release.

In verses seven and eight the author pictures the forgiven saint, thoroughly anchored in a loving God, turning with joy to become an evangelist. He has found so much that satisfies his own soul he wants others to have the same solace and strength and hope. He is thrilled by the pull of his anchor. Why not tell others of its matchless security? He knows the forgiving heart of his eternal Lover. He wants others to know Him and experience that forgiveness. He can reach out and feel the encircling arms of his Keeper while he waits patiently for the morning. Surely he must help others know and have such hope. The joy that is in his soul is unspeakably precious. Surely he must go out of his way to tell others of this abounding joy. The strength gathered from the presence of his divine Keeper is available for all. He will spend his all in telling the good news.

His message to others is the old, old story of plenteous salvation for all. He was thrilled when that consciousness came into his mind. We are told that John Wesley was swept by this marvelous realization while he sat in St. Paul's Cathedral in London listening to the choir present this psalm in song. His heart was stirred to its depths. He was unable to remain to the end of the service. He rushed out into the street to think and to pray and to dedicate himself to a life of preaching the gospel to the masses. He could not hold himself back. The plenteous grace that is available for every creature who will accept it from God's outstretched hand is our treasure today. That realization would send the most timid of us out to be a flaming evangelist. No wonder John Wesley poured forth such streams of eloquent appeal until men and women in all parts of the world felt their hearts melt under the challenge to come to take from this boundless fountain of grace and pardon. *Plenteous redemption!* What an arresting phrase! There is enough for all, enough for each, enough for me. That simple, yet challenging, thought broke in on my troubled soul and I came to Jesus to find forgiveness and full salvation. These years have revealed even deeper reaches of his marvelous grace. No tongue can tell. No words can describe. No language is adequate. He is my all, my Saviour, my Keeper, my Lord. At His feet I fall in humility, in deep reverence, in full surrender, in wholehearted dedication of myself to keep on telling the only glad news the world has ever heard. I must live for Him. I must praise Him. I must reveal to others what that poor soul needs. No words can describe the joy that is mine as I realize the fullness of His grace and the privilege that is mine to tell His story.

> Plenteous grace with Thee is found,
> Grace to cover all my sin:
> Let the healing streams abound;
> Make me, keep me pure within.
> Thou of life the fountain art,
> Freely let me take of Thee;
> Spring Thou up within my heart,
> Rise to all eternity.

Even as the Shepherd reached down His strong arms to lift the exhausted Psyche from the mire and brought life to her, so will our good Shepherd hear the cry of any helpless suppliant and come with love and mercy and forgiveness to make possible a life with Him throughout earth's brief sojourn and then throughout the endless ages of an eternity on the other shore. So many are in the depths. They do not know the Saviour. They will never find the salvation that can bring earth's sweetest joys until one of us goes with gentleness and love to tell them of the love of our Lord and Saviour. How can we wait longer to tell them of this amazing grace? Remember the picture of Jesus that He loved best of all the collection of portraits. Was it not the picture of the good Shepherd who gladly gave himself to the last ounce of his energy to rescue a thoughtless sheep? It has been the favorite story in our family circle all through the life of our youngsters. Each child would sit with breathless attention as the intriguing details of the story unfolded. No night could pass without the telling. Each one learned to repeat the graphic language. A holy hush fell over each one as the little minds grasped the eternal pathos of the drama. Is it any wonder that when the youngest of them was asked, at the age of sixteen, to give a devotional message before a large group of adults, she began with the familiar details of this absorbing narrative. She had learned as a baby girl the sweetness and beauty of the love of her good Shepherd. He is ever precious to those who have given heart and life to Him.

In the great revival in the British Isles a grand old Welsh preacher translated verse four *There is forgiveness with thee—enough to frighten us!* It is truly the deepest note in all the story of redemption. How the lost, needy, dying multitudes need to know this truth! No other Saviour can be found. No other remedy will avail. No other way will be open. He is the way, the truth, the life. He will reach down into the depths and lift the sinful soul out of the clutches of death and provide forgiveness, cleansing, restoration, a new heart and music for the starved soul. Why not tell them of His love, His willingness to forgive, His power to save, His rich gifts for hungry hearts?

XII

TWO PORTRAITS—TWO WAYS

PSALM 1

Blessed is the man who walks not in the counsel of the ungodly, nor stands in the way of sinners, nor sits in the seat of the scornful. But his delight is in the law of the Lord; and in his law he meditates day and night. And he shall be like a tree planted by the rivers of water, which yields its fruit in its season; his leaf also shall not wither: and whatsoever he does shall prosper. The ungodly are not so; but are like the chaff which the wind drives away. Therefore the ungodly shall not stand in the judgment, nor sinners in the congregation of the righteous. For the Lord knows the way of the righteous; but the way of the ungodly shall perish.

WOULD it interest you to know that Jesus reached back into Psalm I for the text for His immortal sermon on the mount? When He needed a great text for His inaugural message He found it in this psalm. To these disciples He preached an expository sermon using the main outline of this ancient poem. In that sermon He pictured the ideal kingdom man and developed four definite thoughts: his character, his influence, his conduct, and his destiny. Jesus knew the message of this great psalm and boldly adapted it to the men who listened as He preached. He realized that the man who ignores God or shuts Him out of his life is on the road to ruin and eternal death. He taught that life must have some strong refusals and also some great positives.

How Jesus longed to see men live the abundant life and drink in the rich joys that were eternally available! He says: *I came that ye might have life and have it more abundantly.*

The psalm has been called "the threshold psalm" for it forms such an ideal portal to the sanctuary of the Psalter. It constitutes a perfect epitome of the whole book. In it we find an Old Testament sermon on the blessedness of the life that is wholly committed to God and the utter destruction that awaits the one who leaves God out of consideration. The only way that a man can hope to have enduring happiness is to be found in fellowship with God. He alone can give the rich blessings that every soul has a right to enjoy. At the very entrance to the Psalms, we are confronted with a solemn call to conduct a rigid self-examination. The author regards it of such importance that he insists on having us face the test and settle our standing before God. Inner motives, desires, yearnings, and thoughts must be subjected to the glaring light of God's own testing. Two portraits are painted for us. One of them is finished fully and completely. The canvas is turned and the other striking picture takes shape before us. One picture is the exact opposite of the other. In choice, in character, in influence, in conduct, and in final destiny, the contrast is carried out with clean strokes of a master hand. Only six brief verses are used, but there is no feeling of haste or incompleteness. The work is beautifully done. The author knows that three perils threaten human beings. He urges his readers to guard their direction, their leisure, and their company. What a difference it would make in the life of our people if these three matters could be closely guarded! How carefully the youth of our land should heed this word of wisdom!

CERTAIN REFUSALS

This man was an alert man. He understood how tremendously important refusals may be in the building of character. There are certain things that he simply cannot do. A few powerful stakes must be driven down. With clear, incisive mind he thought straight through the problems that faced him. No weak drifting was to characterize his journey through life. Courage and determination and bold aggressiveness were in evidence at every turn in the road. With keen insight, he thought through all the paths and estimated the dangers, the pitfalls, the perils, as well as the highways to happiness and victory. With a positive hatred for persons and ways and things that are opposed to God, he deliberately set himself against doing certain things. In the light of all these considerations he set up three definite refusals to guide his way.

1. *Walking in the counsel of the ungodly.* He refuses to expose himself to the ideas and attitudes of the men who have no place for God in their thoughts and in their lives. He will avoid getting counsel from men who do not love and reverence God. He realizes that it is a tragic hour for a young man when he begins getting his slant on life from ungodly men. Unfortunately there are many who take peculiar delight in giving to immature youth a brand of worldly philosophy that hurts instead of helps. Happy is the man who habitually avoids places where the atmosphere is not conducive to wholesome thinking and high living. In some cities there are certain sections that are declared "out of bounds" for our soldiers and sailors. How many places do you know where conditions are such that a similar ruling ought to be made for all our people? Evil companions start a young man on the downward road away from God and right and decency. Not until it is too late does he realize the

deadly harm that is being brought upon him. The psalmist pictures the man who has, with resolute heart, set himself against the very beginning of such a course. He will not walk in the general direction of evil. He will not allow wicked companions to find him in a place where their work with him will be easy.

2. *Standing in the way of sinners.* He refuses to stop and associate himself with rebellious offenders. Men who spend their time blocking the progress of the kingdom cannot count on him. He will not go to their houses. He will watch his leisure hours and be careful where he loiters. He realizes the deadly drag that can come to his spiritual conceptions, his convictions, and his high resolves if he submits to the influence of such men. He is keen enough to know how they can hurt him. In order that he may keep himself free from such influences, he deliberately sets himself to avoid these men as he would flee the plague. He does not want his moral sense blunted and dulled as it will inevitably be in such atmosphere. The prophet Hosea describes that tragic matter as sin "cutting the optic nerve" of the soul. Sin and pagan atmosphere can make the conscience flabby and weak and render it ineffective. The powers of spiritual discernment are weakened so that it is difficult to make moral distinctions. How tragic it is to find men and women who have allowed sin to rob them of the power of discernment. Once they were keen and alert and sensitive to moral distinctions, but now all powers of deciding ethical questions have been dissipated. This ideal young man is definitely set to avoid loitering in places where he can be hurt by men who do not love and reverence God. No siren call to be led astray to waste his God-given talents and to blunt his spiritual perception can be tolerated by him. He refuses to have anything to do with such individuals. To "stand" in the company of sinners would indicate he had lost some of his sensitiveness

to sin and that he is being brought under the spell of sin. It is the picture of the bird who is gradually drawn nearer and nearer to the mouth of the snake.

3. *Sitting in the seat of scorners.* He refuses to sit down with those who sneer and scoff at truth and sacred things. Deliberate association with those who openly mock at religion is not worthy of his time and attention. The "synod of the cynic" is to be avoided since it can but hurt and hinder and weaken. The cynic is a chronic sufferer. His heart is soured. He has no respect for anything that is high or holy or sacred. He snaps, growls, bites, and snarls as a lowbred dog. A group made up of such persons is a dangerous group. The godly man says, "I will not join such an unholy crowd."

We have seen that the ideal man refuses to *walk* by, *stand* with, or *take his seat* in the company of those who will pull him down and make his influence of less value. In that brief verse we have the three successive steps in a career of evil portrayed. The foolish one might walk by a questionable place without any intention of going into sin. He merely wants to see what it is like. The next step is to loiter around long enough to let evil get its grip on him. He is now warming himself at the fire of the enemy. He is learning to like the things he hears, sees, and experiences. The next step is to walk boldly into a group of blatant enemies of the true and sacred and ask for membership in the society of scorners. When a man begins the life of sin, he goes easily from bad to worse. The road is down hill all the way. The godly man has set himself against even the earliest tendency in that direction. Our young people need to be led to see the urgent need for definite refusals in their lives. The backbone is even more useful than the wishbone. Wrecks and tragedies can be avoided by wise decisions.

Yield not to temptation, For yielding is sin;
Each vict'ry will help you Some other to win;
Fight manfully onward, Dark passions subdue,
Look ever to Jesus, He'll carry you through.

THE POSITIVE PRINCIPLE

How can a man be strong enough to do what the godly
man has done? What is the secret? Is he a man whose life is
ruled by negatives? Does he react to successive "don'ts"?
What gives him the courage and power to build such a life?
The psalmist reveals the secret. His heart and interests and
affections are somewhere else. He is in love with One who
exerts a stronger influence over him. He is unwilling to have
the keen, sharp edge of his soul blunted by unholy associa-
tions. He will not let his soul be soiled by the slurs and
cynical remarks of ungodly men. He says, "That is not my
life." *His delight is in the Torah of the Lord.* His heart is
elsewhere. The Word of God is not only the rule of his
conduct, it is to him a delightful morsel of food for his soul
and mind. He enjoys the taste, the exhilarating effect, the
soul-satisfying nourishment. It is food for his hungry soul.
It enriches, broadens, nourishes, and quickens his capacities.
He has learned to love what God says and what God wills
for his life. There are some "don'ts" in his life because there
are other things he would rather do. He recognizes that his
body is *the temple of the Holy Spirit*, and it is his delight to
learn and think on God's will for his life.

What are the consequences? As a result of such refusals
and such delights, we find that he is *like a tree planted.* He
has vitality, fertility, steadfastness, security, freshness, fruit-
fulness, charm, and unending prosperity, because of his love
for the Lord and the divine will for his life. He is like the
stately palm tree whose roots go deep into the earth to find
life from the eternal fountains that give life and freshness.

Rooted, steadfast, fixed, anchored, he rides out the storm unmoved and stronger than ever. Fed and nourished from an unending fountain of rich treasures, he finds new freshness and growth. The natural result is a vigorous, productive, fruit-bearing tree that is the delight of its owner. Such a life will be eternally prosperous and happy and fruitful. The secret of his success is found in the reserves that have been built in and stored up for the hours of testing. He has access to reservoirs that do not dry up. He is rich in life that abides. *He bringeth forth his fruit in his season.* Sorrow, distress, misfortune, and seeming failure only cause him to dig deeper into his inexhaustible supply of rich treasures that are always available.

Is this a photograph of your own self? As you analyze your store of resources, do you find them adequate? Are you anchored to the Rock? Have you found in Him the sources of strength that give you moral stamina and courage to carry on in the dark hour when distress and anguish come to shake the soul? Can you face the storms of life with the assurance that a plentiful supply of riches has been stored up for your own use? Are you in touch with His vast sea of life-giving riches so that you may stand in the hour of testing? *If thou hast run with the footmen, and they have wearied thee, then how canst thou contend with horses? and if in the land of peace, wherein thou trustedst, they wearied thee, then how wilt thou do in the swelling of Jordan?*

THE UNGODLY ARE NOT SO

The psalmist uncovers the reverse side of the canvas now and reveals to us a striking contrast. The man who has willed to live by his own will instead of by the will of God stands before us as the exact opposite of the godly man on the other side. We now see the character, the conduct, and the destiny of a man who chose to keep God out of his life. He is not a

tree that can defy the storm and continue to grow, to bear
fruit, to abide in rich beauty, but a bit of worthless chaff
that is not only worthless but utterly helpless before the fury
of the same storm that blew upon the tree. He is dead, dry,
wind-driven, insecure, helpless, short-lived chaff, with no
hope of permanence, or fruit, or attractiveness, or freshness,
or stability. His way comes to naught because it is essentially
godless. In Job 6:18 a caravan is described as going up into
the waste places of the desert following streams that promise
sustenance. Death comes to all of them because these streams
on which they depended were dried up by the intense heat.
How true to life even in our day! How easy it is for men and
women to live a godless life, running feverishly on in pursuit of ephemeral things that will pass away in the hour of
deepest need. Jeremiah describes the tragic career of thoughtless men who turned from God to useless pursuits. *For my
people have committed two evils; they have forsaken me the
fountain of living waters, and hewed them out cisterns,
broken cisterns, that can hold no water.*

The real character of the ungodly man is manifested in
the hour of judgment. *The wind drives it away.* Doom is inevitable. The house is built on the sand. No foundation is
available in the storm. It is helplessly driven before the cruel
wind. The inexhaustible rivers of life-giving strength are
near but chaff does not have roots that can reach into the
fountain of life. How unspeakably pathetic! The man who
has tried to get through the world without God now finds
that he has lost the one treasure among all the rich treasures
of time and eternity. He put all his treasure in a place *where
moth and rust corrupt and where thieves break through and
steal.* At the end of the way, he finds that he has no permanence, no anchor, no rock, no home, no God, no light at
eventide. He that stands in the way of sinners shall not stand
in the judgment. He will be there and will face the righteous

Judge, but his flimsy excuses will not help him in the hour of deepest need. He cannot count on the Advocate to plead for him because he lived his life on earth without any surrender to the great Redeemer who wanted to be his Saviour and Advocate.

Thus we have a picture of every life that seeks to grovel along without God and is not rooted and grounded in Him. The psalmist tells us in his final summary (6) that *the Lord knows*—He takes note and rewards accordingly. The direction and way of the life is watched, guarded, approved, blessed, or condemned, according to a divine standard. He is the perfect Judge who can look into the deepest heart and judge with absolute equity. *The path of the just is as a shining light which shineth more and more till the noontide of the day. The way of the wicked is as darkness—they know not at what they stumble.* Can you imagine a more poignant prospect? How can any man neglect the preparation that will fit him to enjoy the endless joys that God has provided for those who love Him?

APPLICATION

Have you followed the suggestion made by the author? Do you see your portrait? What of your life? Will you be frank and honest with yourself and look at your character, your influence, your conduct, and your final destiny? So much depends on your choice now. Your eternal destiny is at stake. Have you chosen to let God rule your life? Have you given back to Him the keys to all the rooms in your heart? Can you honestly say that you belong to Him? If not, please, for your own sake, get on your knees in a quiet place of prayer and surrender everything to Him. Nothing else matters unless that question is settled right. If you are truly His and can claim Jesus Christ as your own personal Saviour, then all life is different. These refusals will be easy. These delights will be natural delights. You will be vitally connected with Him. You can say with Paul, *Nay, in all these things we are more than conquerors through him that loved us,* and have the power to make it true, remembering in it all Jesus' words to His disciples, *and, lo, I am with you always.* When the end of this brief bit of earthly existence comes you will find life just beginning, so full, so rich, so satisfying that joy unspeakable will be yours. Remember our Lord's words to His friends, *In my Father's house are many mansions: if it were not so, I would have told you. I go to prepare a place for you. And if I go and prepare a place for you, I will come again, and receive you unto myself; that where I am, there ye may be also.* The Saviour will be your Advocate and you will be ushered into an eternal round of joy and heavenly delights. May His Spirit lead you to surrender your life to Him in fullest devotion.

XIII

GOD'S ANOINTED KING

PSALM 2

Why do the nations rage, and the peoples imagine a vain thing?
The kings of the earth set themselves, and rulers take counsel
together, against the Lord, and against his Anointed, saying,
Let us break their bands asunder, and cast away their cords from
us. He that sits in the heavens will laugh. The Lord will have them
in derision. Then will he speak to them in his wrath, and vex
them in his hot displeasure. Yet have I set my King upon my holy
hill of Zion. I will declare the decree. The Lord said to me, Thou
art my Son; this day have I begotten thee. Ask of me, and I will
give the heathen for thine inheritance, and the ends of the earth
for thy possession. . . . Be wise now therefore, O ye kings; be
instructed, ye judges of the earth. . . . Kiss the Son, lest he be
angry, and ye perish in the way, when his wrath is kindled but a
little. Blessed are all they that put their trust in him.

THIS remarkable lyric has no equal when one seeks for a
poem that carries a pictorial presentation of so much in
a few words. The terse, vivid, compact treatment keeps the
imagination on the jump. Speakers change without warning.
The scene shifts quickly and dramatically. The four stanzas
of three verses each are closely related and yet each is distinct
and different. The author has kept the artistic balance so
perfectly that each stanza contains practically the same number of words. Each picture is perfectly finished without the

slightest hint of hurry or crowding. It is a masterpiece. The psalm is prophecy as well as poetry. Its theme is a real person.

Interpreters have sought diligently for the king of Israel represented in this psalm. David has been considered and Solomon's name has been urged as meeting the conditions. Some earthly king is needed who ran into the difficulty pictured here. Soon after his ascension to the throne all the subject nations sought to throw off the yoke and assert their independence. It is difficult to find records of such revolts in the life of either of these men. Something approximating these conditions might have been true in either reign. It is not necessary, however, to settle the issue since the evident purpose of the author is to refer to the ideal King who was to come as the Messiah of Jewish hope. Perhaps some historical occasion suggested the psalm but its language and scope of understanding far transcends any actual earthly experience.

Kirkpatrick says: "The Psalm then is typical and prophetic of the rebellion of the kingdoms of the world against the kingdom of Christ, and of the final triumph of the kingdom of Christ. To Him all nations are given for an inheritance; if they will not submit He must judge them."[1]

In the *first stanza* (1-3) a picture of *world-wide rebellion* is painted. With the color and vividness of an eyewitness he not only describes the scenes but breaks forth in astonishment and surprise at the incredible things he sees. There is wild commotion as nations and peoples rush madly to one central meeting place. Mob psychology has its inning. Everyone is upset and bothered. It is clearly a meeting designed to stir up a revolt. Rumors and charges and plots fly thick and fast. The air is charged with electricity. The spark to set off the conflagration seems ready for the zero hour. Messengers have

[1] *The Psalms*, p. 7.

rounded up highly excitable peoples from all the subject peoples. Our poet gives utterance to an indignant and astonished *why*. Their revolt is groundless and hopeless. Why should men be so silly?

In the second verse the picture is changed enough to show the kings in their secret assembly. While the growls of discontent continue on the outside these rulers are sitting in special session to plot revolt and treason. Right before our eyes these changes are taking place. By means of changes in tenses the poet lets us in on the rapid movement in minds and on the ground. They are plotting treason. They are subjects of the king and owe him their allegiance. But in secret plot and in open rebellion they are seeking to throw off the yoke and paddle their own canoes. They will not let the bands and cords control or guide them. They seek freedom. Their hearts are full of passion and hatred but they must be cautious. It is a perilous thing they are plotting. Finally they seem agreed. They will break bands and cast away cords. The die is cast. It is an hour of crisis.

They were actually rebelling against the Lord and His Anointed. It was a serious matter. It was utterly hopeless. How could they hope to break bands and cords and loose restraints? It is the same thing that we see in our day. Jesus spoke of it in His day when He pictured the prodigal son seeking the far country where he could be free. It was the very thing he failed to find. Only as he came back to the father's house did he find the freedom he had sought.

In the *second stanza* (4-6) we catch a glimpse of *divine indignation*. The scene has changed and the rebellious assembly is left behind while we look in on the heavenly scene. Instead of wild, frenzied excitement we see a picture of calm dignity. He is not afraid. There is no cause for alarm even though all these princes have plotted against Him and against His Son, the newly crowned King. Why should He be alarmed? He is secure in His eternal abode. No harm can come to Him or to His kingdom.

The poet uses a bold figure to describe God's behavior. He says, *He that sits in the heavens laughs.* Imagine the boldness of such a statement! What a contrast with the stir, the passion, the wild talk, the senseless decisions, and the unfounded charges! The divine calm expresses itself in a quiet laugh. He is but indicating the utter futility of such folly. It is not that He was unconcerned or uninterested in bringing them back to their senses. It is not at all inconsistent with the picture of love for all men. He loved these rebellious ones as devotedly as His great heart ever loved any other creature.

The prophet Habakkuk accused God of showing no interest in his problems. The charge almost went to the point of accusing God of doing a poor job of running the world. He was either asleep or uninterested or unable to do anything about it. Here we find men who think they can break away and exert their own powers to end their bondage to One who fails to please them as a Sovereign.

Following the laugh there are three other words that reveal volumes concerning God. The words are *derision, wrath, displeasure.* It seems that He is thoroughly aroused. It is not enough for Him to laugh a quiet, secure laugh because of the absence of fear and alarm. He is aroused because of the sin that has been openly displayed. It is a serious crime to rebel against God. His wrath burns and He utters a word that throws the little assembly into confusion and despair. By gentle patience He has dealt with these rebels for a long time. The time has come for powerful speech. They must be silenced. It is a terrible thing to have God against you.

The closing sentence comes as a mighty pronouncement from the throne. *I have set my King upon my holy hill of Zion.* The pronoun is emphatic. This news is enough to silence any opposition. No longer can they be so senseless as to rebel against this anointed One for He is appointed by the eternal God Himself.

In the *third stanza* (7-9) we hear the Anointed interpreting the *great declaration*. The Son is thrilled by the decree that the Father has just spoken. It is now His turn to speak. The scene is either in the heavens near the Father's throne or on earth at the head of His army in a last minute effort to bring about a truce that will lead to peace. It seems plausible to think of it in the earthly setting. The Anointed speaks of God's choice of Him as the ruler who should carry out the divine plans for His creatures. That plan involved judgment, chastisement, warfare against the evil forces, and the ultimate victory that would make it possible for the bound ones of the earth to be free to come home with Him again. He makes it quite clear that He is the Son and that the Father has given to Him a marvelous birthday gift. He declares that God said to Him, *Ask of me and I will give the heathen for thine inheritance, and the uttermost parts of the earth for thy possession.* His gift is a universal kingdom with people who can be led to bow down before Him and accept Him as their Ruler and Lord. What a glorious vista is opened up before Him! Nations and peoples of every land will be His! The implied condition is an added **challenge, for the** Messiah gladly welcomes the order to go out and win them. It will not be easy. Terrific warfare must be waged. A fanatical foe must be met and outsmarted and defeated. The satanic power of this foe must be destroyed. Death must come to provide the atonement that will guarantee victory. The debt must be paid. The ransom must be provided. The cruel devil must be tracked down to his lair and destroyed.

After His resurrection His eternal sonship will be fully recognized (Acts 13:33). The missionary activity must bring about the evangelization of the nations of the earth. Before going home to the Father, Jesus said: *All power is given unto me in heaven and in earth. Go ye, therefore, and teach all nations, baptizing them in the name of the Father, and of the Son, and of the Holy Ghost; teaching them to observe all things whatsoever I have commanded you; and, lo, I am with you always, even unto the end of the world. But ye shall receive power, after that the Holy Ghost is come upon you; and ye shall be witnesses unto me both in Jerusalem, and in all Judea, and in Samaria, and unto the uttermost part of the earth.* His work was to be a mission of conquest. Figures are used in this psalm to indicate rough tactics are to be employed, but it is thoroughly clear that our Lord interpreted His mission in the terms of His farewell messages to His followers. Nations and peoples were to hear the Word, learn of His sacrifice, see something of the depths of His love and then come in penitence to Him for cleansing and forgiveness and salvation. It was God's way. It is His way for us. May we listen as He urges us to go out into all the world to make disciples of all peoples and thus help Him win *the nations for His inheritance and the uttermost parts of the earth for His possession.* What joy it will be to see the Son coming in to present His blood-bought trophies to His Father! How glorious it will be that He has won them! Through toil and pain and suffering and death He went to make it possible for them to come home with Him to the Father's house. Some of us can rejoice in the thought that we have been saved and that we have actually helped our Lord with His mission.

In the *fourth stanza* (10-12) the poet gives a *solemn exhortation* to the kings and judges of the earth. In the light of all that has been disclosed he has a word of wisdom for all of them. The facts are before them. They can now see how silly it would be to rebel against the Lord and His Anointed.

They must face the true situation. Caution and reflection and wise behavior must be their choice for the coming days. All other kings and princes must take account of the serious nature of the problem. He urges wise consideration of the consequences of rebellion.

They will hasten to Him in full acknowledgment of His right to reign if they are wise. The words "kiss the son" may best be rendered "embrace instruction." The word translated "son" is an Aramaic word. Whatever the translation, the meaning is clear. The poet is seeking to get all men to bow in homage and loyalty to the Anointed One lest the Lord bring well-deserved blows upon them. His Son is the King and to refuse to be loyal to Him is rebellion against the Lord's will and authority. The psalm makes it clear that the Lord and the Son are one in their rule over men. It is the Lord's anger that flashes forth upon rebellious subjects but it is always the result of men's rebellion against His Son. The one divine concern seems to be that men may accept the rule and leading of the Son. They sin against God when they refuse to bow in full surrender to the Anointed One. The poet has grasped one of the deepest truths of the Bible. It comes out more clearly in the New Testament. Jesus sought to convince men that He and the Father were one and that He was but working out the divine will on earth. *He that hath seen me hath seen the Father. Believe me that I am in the Father, and the Father in me.*

The sentence, *and ye perish in the way for quickly may His anger blaze forth,* is not one to be passed over without full consideration. Too often we lose sight of this tragic truth in our eagerness to emphasize the love of God. The word "perish" is the same word that forms the dark background for John 3:16. Only with the stark reality of that background before us can we see and appreciate the beauty of God's love. Men will perish if they persist in rebellion against God. That rebellion is expressed when they refuse to acknowledge and love the Son. No truth is clearer in the gospel. No other sin is needed to bring the wrath of God on a soul. Jesus said: *He that believeth not is condemned already because he hath not believed on the only begotten Son of God. He that disbelieves the Son shall not see life, but the wrath of God abideth on him.* It is tragically true. God's wrath will blaze forth. You may call it cruel or lacking in love or unfair or anything you like, but the Word of God unhesitatingly states it as a fact. A righteous Father must be true to the principles of justice and holiness that lie deepest in His being. The wrath of God must blaze forth against sin. It is only as the Son takes the blazing fury of that wrath upon His own innocent person and becomes the sinless Substitute that anyone can hope to escape the fiery blast. The psalmist is true to rebellious men when he faithfully warns against the deadliest sin of all. Let them consider seriously the tragic consequences of rebellion against God's beloved Son.

> Let ev'ry kindred, ev'ry tribe
> On this terrestrial ball,
> To Him all majesty ascribe,
> And crown Him Lord of all.

True to the nature of a loving God, He will not leave us on that note of wrath and destruction. He is even more concerned than we that the wrath may not need to shoot forth. He does not get any pleasure in seeing men suffer from the divine blasts. *For why will ye die, O house of Israel? For I have no pleasure in the death of him that dieth, saith the Lord God; wherefore turn yourselves, and live.* The whole psalm has been written to produce the kind of response indicated in the last line, *Happy are all they that take refuge in Him.* The blessed alternative is before us. *Trust in Him.* The way to peace and joy and life is thus revealed. Instead of the road to destruction David recommends the way to peace and happy security in Him. The way to rest is beautifully pictured as the flight of the soul to find shelter and safety under the wings of God. The one who trusts the Son need have no fear of the flames of wrath but can know indescribable joys in the presence of God whose wrath has been turned away because of the intercession of the Son who gladly bore the wrath of God to become the Saviour of all who come to Him in faith. It is only by way of loyal and loving submission to Christ that one is ever able to find reconciliation with God. No other way can ever be devised. Calvary speaks its own emphatic word on this subject.

Thus the two notes are beautifully emphasized in this psalm. Revolt brings ruin. Simple trust brings full and free salvation. It is God's will to break the spirit of rebellion in the sinner in order to make him ready for the salvation provided for all men. Only misery can be the portion of one who refuses to let God have His rightful place in the heart and life. It is always a tragic matter when one of God's creatures refuses to love and to serve Him. Trust and surrender will always bring forgiveness and restoration to a place in His favor. Our Father cannot encourage or allow rebellion and sin but He can reveal His own forgiving heart. Those who look into the depths of His heart can learn of the rich depths of love that pour forth to keep and to bless.

> Jesus shall reign where'er the sun
> Does his successive journeys run;
> His kingdom spread from shore to shore,
> Till moons shall wax and wane no more.

XIV

GENUINE THANKSGIVING

PSALM 116

I love the Lord, because he has heard my voice and my supplications. Because he has inclined his ear to me, therefore will I call upon him as long as I live. The sorrows of death encompassed me, and the pains of Sheol took hold upon me. I found trouble and sorrow. Then called I upon the name of the Lord; O Lord, I beseech thee, deliver my soul. I was brought low, and he helped me. Return unto thy rest, O my soul; for the Lord has dealt bountifully with thee. For thou hast rescued my soul from death, my eyes from tears, and my feet from falling. I will walk before the Lord in the land of the living. . . . What shall I render unto the Lord for all his benefits toward me? I will take the cup of salvation, and call upon the name of the Lord. I will pay my vows unto the Lord now in the presence of all his people. . . . I will offer to thee the sacrifice of thanksgiving, and will call upon the name of the Lord. I will pay my vows to the Lord now in the presence of all his people. In the courts of the Lord's house, in the midst of thee, O Jerusalem. Praise ye the Lord.

ALL the world loves a lover." Would you like to see how a lover seeks to prove his love? This psalmist has fallen in love with God and declares that he is ready to commit himself without reservation to the kind of life that will be an eloquent announcement of what love can do in a heart. Would you know the secret? Will you look upon him and listen to his earnest declarations? You will like him so much that you might follow him in prayer, in obedient walk, in generous giving, and in jubilant praise.

He is not complaining but we soon learn that he has suffered severely. He found himself on the very edge of the precipice, in the strong grip of disease, bowed in anguish and grief, broken and lonely and almost without hope or faith. In that tragic plight he turned his faint cry to God with a feeble faith and a flickering hope. God heard him and came with such a marvelous deliverance that he now finds himself deeply in debt to the gracious Deliverer. In the light of this experience gratitude wells up within him and from those springs he is constrained to bring the purest and best to his Lover Friend who has wrought so bountifully. In the psalm he recounts for us the many blessings he has received and states the response his heart will make to God.

His psalm is a beautiful word of thanksgiving. We cannot read it without being stirred to count our own blessings and, out of sheer gratitude, pour out our promises to such a bountiful giver. Some signal deliverance has revealed the depths of divine mercy. In thinking on it the poet promises to pray to God (1-8), engage in holy conversation (9-13), and to commit his whole life to praise and worship and service (14-19). He records the motives and reasons that prompt him to embark on such an unusual pilgrimage. Gratitude impels him to express in thought, in word, and in deed, the deep response of his overflowing heart. Men may know that he is in love with God and that he is devoting his best love and service to the giver of all good blessings.

In the first verse he says: *I love the Lord.* In verse two he promises prayer: *I will call on the Lord.* In the ninth verse he resolves on a life of holy walking: *I will walk before the Lord.* These three things are sufficient to challenge the best in any man. The devotion of the soul, the words of the mouth, one's daily behavior, are elements that bring joy to the heart of God. In genuine life he devotes his best thoughts to the doing of that which his God desires. He knows God, loves God, belongs to God, recognizes that he has been signally blessed by the divine hand, offers to pay vows to God, and promises that his testimony will be filled with praise and thanksgiving as long as he lives. It will help us to study carefully the words as the psalmist names the things God had done for him and records the promises he makes to God.

I LOVE

That simple statement reveals a world of truth. The person who has genuine love in his heart is capable of depths and heights and qualities that may well call forth our admiration. The correct translation is: *I love, because Jehovah hears my voice, even my supplication.* Naturally the object of that love is Jehovah so it is all right to translate it: *I love Jehovah for he hears my voice, my supplication.* The meaning is the same for we see the psalmist as a lover. He is desperately in love with God. We shall not be surprised at anything good in his life after this declaration.

When Jesus was seeking to get a fast grip on Simon Peter He did not inquire about his creed, his orthodoxy, his conduct, his faithfulness, but did dig in with a question that came three times: *Lovest thou me?* He remembered that Peter had failed Him in that bitter experience because love was lacking. Where there is love all these other things will be right. A wife does not have to ask a half dozen questions about her husband's conduct and generosity when she has the true answer to the question: "Do you love me?" The psalmist has unconsciously revealed everything in this very first line. He is a lover. That love is for his God. We already know the outcome even here at the beginning.

What God Has Done for Me

In this brief psalm he recounts for us some of the good things God has done for him. Perhaps we can find in these words the picture of God's dealing with us. Surely He has been good to us. It will help us to pause long enough to count our blessings. What has the Lord done for you? It is interesting to know that the word "think" is strangely akin to the word "thank." When we think we thank.

1. *He inclined His ear* (2). It is difficult for any one of us to appreciate fully the quality of the divine love that makes our Father willing to turn His ear in our direction so that even the faint prayer of a feeble sufferer or a young child can be clearly heard and understood. It is the picture of a kind physician who puts his ear very close to the mouth of the sufferer in order to hear the slightest request, or of a busy father who never fails to pause to lean over when a toddling son wants to speak something in his ear. It is simple but exceedingly profound. Our Father in heaven would have us think of Him in this way and be conscious of the divine love that prompts such infinite tenderness. He loves us more than we can ever know.

2. *He heard my voice and my supplications* (1). The Hebrew verb means more than our English verb "hear." The psalmist says that God not only inclined His ear but He heard and answered His servant's pleading. It is a picture of a gracious Answerer who makes it possible for the petitions to have an answer. Our Father is anxious to know our wants and our needs. He is always ready to provide even more generously than we imagined. He suffers when we do not pray to Him. Why is it that so many of us refuse to give God a chance to enrich our lives, deliver us from suffering, save us from defeat, and give us the joys that He alone can give? The poet is giving the picture of a loving Father who hears

the cry, inclines the ear, understands the request, and graciously gives the answer. He has unlimited supplies from which to draw the gifts. His love for His children makes Him anxious to have them enjoy His treasures.

3. *He delivered me* (6-8). He describes to us something of his condition when he turned to God in prayer. He tells us that the cords of death were wrapped about him to render him helpless. As hunters surround a stag with men and dogs so that no way of escape is left so was he hemmed in. Another figure describes the horrors of Sheol as taking hold of him so that fears and agonies and sufferings made life utterly miserable for him. It is a horrible experience that calls forth fervent prayers. From such unspeakable terrors the mighty arm of God snatched him. He is now free from the clutches of despair and suffering. It is a wise man who understands the solace and strength and forgiveness that may come to one so sorely pressed if he will only fall back upon the loving arms of the great Deliverer.

He finds that God has dealt bountifully with him. As the blessings are numbered, one by one, he is amazed at the number and the richness of them. God has been too good to him. If that were true for the Old Testament saint how much more is there for us to count and appreciate. He has given us His own Son as a Saviour and Redeemer and through Him we become heirs of God. He has sent us the Holy Spirit who brings to us all spiritual blessings. By day and by night *He has dealt bountifully with us.*

In verse six the psalmist tells us that he was *brought low.* Affliction and trial did their worst and he was severely broken. The word literally means "to be drawn dry." The metaphor pictures a pond or a brook that is completely exhausted or dried up. The man is helpless. Anything done for him will have to be the help given by the divine hand. From that distress he was mercifully delivered and new life came to make him strong to go on again.

In verse eight he reveals God's marvelous salvation from *death*, from *tears*, from *falling*. Death is vanquished, tears are dried, and fears are banished when the Lord is near. The word translated "deliver" is the same verb that is so often translated "save." It is the root verb for the name Joshua or Jesus. Jehovah has indeed proved Himself a Saviour to our psalmist. The further he goes in counting his blessings the bigger the debt becomes. He has received so many rich blessings from the hand of God that he will never be able to express all the gratitude that is due. How can he prove to the Lord that he really has gratitude in his heart? What can he do to express his thanks to God?

What Shall I Do For Him?

Love prompts the lover to do something for the one loved. What foolish things young lovers have done in buying expensive rings and gifts to be lavished upon the objects of their love! How clear it is that a real love burns in the heart! Love causes the lover to give. Our psalmist gives utterance to some of his resolutions. Hear him as he tells what he is going to do to assure God of his unending love.

1. *I will take the cup of salvation* (13). The psalmist has learned the secret of the best way to thank God. There dawns in his heart the discovery that the way that God would have us react to His goodness is to open the heart wider to receive even more. The answer of a grateful heart includes the hearty and instant acceptance of God's salvation. The mercy which He holds out to needy souls will be enthusiastically received. It is God's will that all His mercies shall find their way into the glorious work of redeeming, transforming, and ennobling human hearts and lives. Our psalmist is going to be one

who will keep his heart and mind and soul and body for every touch of God so that he may not only be stronger and happier but that he will be able to carry out God's will for his life. He will accept the full salvation provided, the sure guidance, the adequate remedy, the Holy Spirit's sanctification, and the eternal life made available for all those who will take from God's hand the blessed cup of salvation. Can we ever know the joy that comes to the heart of God when a needy soul agrees to accept from the merciful hand all the wondrous blessings which He has in store for all men? What tragedies we find on every hand when creatures made in the image of God refuse to take the cup of salvation and make it possible for a loving Father to work out His plan! What will eternity reveal of tragedy and gain?

2. *I will call upon the name of the Lord* (13, 17). In order to help God work out His perfect work in his life he will set himself to the high privilege of fervent prayer. No food is as nourishing as the soul food that comes through fervent communion with God in prayer. It is the only road to peace and spiritual power. It is God's chosen way for the growing of a great soul. It is the path that provides protection and power and guidance and salvation for others because we pray for them. The author is wise in his decision. He will keep himself close to God by continuous prayer. He will grow a great soul. The unlimited resources of his God are to be at his call. A great life is to be the result.

The Hebrew verb includes more than prayer. It can be translated *proclaim* and be used to describe the activity of the psalmist in acknowledging Jehovah as the giver of all the gifts and blessings. He will not only pray to his God but will spend a good portion of his time telling others of the glorious name of Jehovah. He will be a living witness of all God's gracious dealings.

3. *I will walk before the Lord* (9). He is ready to commit

himself to walk among his fellows in the full consciousness
that God is looking on and knowing every thought and word
and deed. It makes a lot of difference when we know that
He is only a fraction of an inch away and that He knows
what we think, what we say, and what we do. Paul says:
*Only let your manner of life be worthy of the gospel of
Christ.* The psalmist is fully committed to the walk that will
please the One who has done so much for him. Nothing low,
or vulgar, or profane, or immoral, or dishonest, or selfish,
or unworthy of His blessed presence, will be tolerated. He
will not only put out of his life those things that displease
his divine Friend but he will deliberately cultivate the things
that will bring peculiar pleasure to His heart. He now belongs to God and his whole being must be under God's control. Every thought and emotion and his will must be subject to the approval of a holy One who has rescued him and
has great plans for his life.

4. *I will pay my vows to the Lord now* (14, 18). The vow
he made in anguish and pain he now sets out to pay in full.
He is ready for immediate performance and he will do it in
public, before all the people. Vows become debts and debts
should be paid. A promise to God is a sacred thing. No one
should deal lightly with the sacredness and the sanctity of
vows made to almighty God. Far too many of us will make
ready vows when we are in extreme peril or in serious illness
or confronted with powerful fears. How many of us recognize those solemn promises and accept the responsibility of
full payment? Do you know of a man who prayed and begged
and promised God that if He would only save his life or the
life of a loved one that he would go to the church and surrender his life to holy living and become an active follower
of the Lord Jesus Christ? When God heard his prayer and
healed him or his loved one, did he carry out his promise to
God and dedicate his life to the Lord Jesus? Some men do.

Some prove false to their God and to the sacred promise made in the hour of danger and anxiety and fear. God have mercy on one who treats lightly his vow to God.

It is to be a public confession. Secret disciples may have a touch with the Lord but they miss the best joys and lose the opportunity to wield an influence for good and for right. The psalmist declares that he will go *now* to the sanctuary and carry out in full the pledge he made in the day when sorrow and death and Sheol awaited him. It was a great resolve.

5. *I will praise the Lord* (17, 19). God has been so good to him that he plans to spend the rest of his life in praise and thanksgiving. Men will know that he has been miraculously and mercifully saved by the hand of God. They will hear day by day the voice of a grateful soul faithfully telling of the saving grace of God. In the secret place of private prayer, in conversation with friends and neighbors, in sacred song, in public testimony, in special gifts and missionary endeavor, he will be found praising God and sending up thanks to Him. He will praise Him for answered prayers, for miraculous deliverances, for daily guidance and nourishment, for sweet fellowship, for the call to be God's servant, for opportunities to work for the Lord, for the power of the Holy Spirit in his ministry, for that blessed hope of the coming of the Saviour, for the eternal home where joys unspeakable will be his, and for the assurance that the Lord will triumph over sin and death and the devil.

In our own lives we can find plenty of reasons for gratitude and the proper incentives for recording vows to God. Can you say, *I love, I trust, I will take, I will pay, I will walk, I will pray, I will praise?* When I needed Him most He was ready to lift me and to heal me and to preserve me. In the light of all His mercy and love nothing must keep back the overflowing wells of gratitude. Sincere, hearty, public worship that shall include all these different elements must characterize my life from this day.

No wonder he uses the word "Hallelujah" at the close. It is his triumphant call to all peoples to join him in exultant praise. "Hallelu" is a verb in the imperative and is translated "praise ye." The word "Jah" is "Jehovah" or "Lord." He calls on all of us to join him in praise.

XV

GOD HEARS AND SAVES

PSALM 107

O Give thanks unto the Lord, for he is good; for his mercy endures forever. Let the redeemed of the Lord say so, whom he has redeemed from the hand of the enemy. . . . They wandered in the wilderness in a solitary way; they found no city to dwell in. Hungry and thirsty, their soul fainted in them. Then they cried unto the Lord in their trouble, and he rescued them out of their distresses. And he led them forth by the right way, that they might go to a city of habitation. . . . Such as sit in darkness and in the shadow of death, being bound in affliction and iron; Because they rebelled against the words of God, and contemned the counsel of the Most High. Then they cried unto the Lord in their trouble, and he saved them out of their distresses. He brought them out of darkness and the shadow of death, and broke their bands asunder. . . . Fools, because of their transgression, and because of their iniquities, are afflicted. Their soul abhors all manner of food, and they draw near to the gates of death. Then they cry to the Lord in their trouble, and he saves them out of their distresses. He sends his word, and heals them and delivers them from their pits. . . . They that go down to the sea in ships, that do business in great waters. For he commands, and raises the stormy wind, which lifts up the waves. They mount up to the heaven, they go down again to the depths: their soul is melted because of trouble. They reel to and fro, and stagger like a drunken man, and are at their wit's end. Then they cry to the Lord in their trouble, and he brings them out of their distresses. He makes the storm a calm, so that the waves are still. So he brings them to their desired haven. . . . Oh that men would praise the Lord for his goodness, and for his wonderful works to the children of men.

REDEMPTION is the theme. What a note! Surely we are to find rich truth here. Jehovah's main business has always been the business of redemption. It cost Him more to redeem lost men than anyone can ever estimate. The cost of the creation of the world was nothing compared with the cost of salvation. His only begotten Son was freely given to provide the salvation that we enjoy. We are called on to utter praise to Him because *He is good.* What is involved in the word "good"? In the Old Testament practically every other attribute of God is wrapped up in that word. It involves all of the rich mercy of God that became active as saving grace. John is to come forward in the New Testament with the word that *God is love.* The psalmist in his own feeble way is saying just that much. In this remarkable poem he gives illustrations of men in distress, helpless and undone, who turned to the Lord in sincere prayer and found in every instance the saving power of God who is *good.* We are taught that men are incurably bent on rebellion and wandering. In every known peril or calamity God has the deliverance that men so sorely need. He wants men to avail themselves of the priceless privilege that His grace has made possible. Whatever the trouble there is but one way out—the way of sincere appeal to God. That way is never a vain way for it is God's nature to hear and to save. That salvation will be immediate and complete. Since God is *good* any person in distress can count on His saving grace in any emergency. Men who have been redeemed should praise the Lord and bring thanks to Him. Deliverance calls for a song of gratitude. Redeemed ones will delight to praise His name. Songs of rejoicing will pour forth from grateful lips.

Israel is in a very real sense the redeemed of the Lord.

They had been homeless and faint and thirsty and lost and in prison and in dire need. Their merciful Redeemer heard their cry and saved them and *led them* by a way they did not know into a city where they found a home, food, rest, and the protecting arm of the divine Saviour. They sinned in rebelling against covenant love and were plunged into captivity and misery again. When they came to themselves and prayed in penitent commitment He came with His mighty arm of deliverance and brought them again into His place of rest and rich blessings. They are now entreated to praise Him for His salvation that has so clearly demonstrated the inner loving-kindness that is always operative.

Not only does this apply to Israel's deliverance from bondage but it describes God's uniform way of dealing with trouble. It is like Him to want to help needy souls. When you find trouble coupled with prayer **and trust,** you will always find victory and deliverance and songs of praise. When men turn to God from misery or pain or terror or danger, **deliverance is** assured and redeemed men must praise the Deliverer. Man's extremity is God's opportunity. God is constantly watching those who travel dangerous ways for the moment of need when a cry in distress may give Him His great opportunity.

The four pictures that pass before us as we read this poem are selected from the wide abundance of the troubles and distresses that afflict mankind. Travelers who have lost their way in tractless deserts, captives who suffer in terrible prisons, sick men barely able to keep out of the grave, and storm-tossed sailors who are helpless before the relentless storm, are representatives from that vast ocean of misery that lies all about us. The same loving Father who eagerly answered the faint cry of a wayward child still listens for the call of desperate men and women. The Good Shepherd still seeks and saves those who give Him the privilege of proving His love.

THE LOST ONES (4-9)

In seeking to picture how uniformly the grace of God behaves the poet selects a group of men lost and wandering in a desert. They thought they knew the way. They lost the track. Try as they would they continued confused and lost. No city or house or oasis was in sight. No hill presented itself as a vantage ground from which to look for familiar marks. The drinking water gave out, food disappeared, exhaustion was gradually coming on, and with it all hope was fast running out. Soon utter gloom would take hold of the souls of men and dark despair would claim his victims. Soon it would be too late to do anything about it. Their situation was already desperate. Recent harrowing experiences related by men who floated on life rafts for days on the sea make this picture even more real to us. None of us will ever know how tragically these men suffered. None will understand the anguish, the thirst, the gradual loss of hope, the exhaustion of all remaining strength until despair held helpless prisoners in its relentless hands.

Fortunately for the lost men in our poem they finally became desperate enough to pray. In their *distress* they turned to God in prayer. What they needed most was a guide. The only *Guide* was listening and waiting to lead them home. How the divine heart yearned for just one cry! Think of the lost ones all about you who do not know the way home. They cannot find it by themselves. They will wander on in hunger and thirst, unsatisfied and heading toward dark despair. They will never know the joys of salvation until someone helps them toward God. Will you remind them of the Guide, their Redeemer, who wants to be their Saviour? Can it be that you are the one individual who will have that opportunity? A life that has left God out always strays from the right road. He will never find the way to the city under his own power. He needs God. Why not "let go, let God"?

God's answer is immediate. The very second the feeble S O S comes from the desert, the great arm of the Good Shepherd is stretched forth to save. With the divine Guide leading fear fades, hope springs, the way appears, the city is soon reached. What a picture of God's grace and mercy! The psalmist would whisper to us today of the Father's willingness to hear and to save.

The Bound Ones (10-16)

The second episode describes for us a group of individuals languishing in prison with suffering and misery as their daily portion. They are not free to live normal lives. Liberty is denied them. This perhaps refers slightly to the prison experiences in Babylon. Those years of bondage are still fresh memories to the redeemed ones. The general structure of the psalm, however, seems to lead us far beyond a local application. It is quite clear that Jehovah is represented as ready for every individual who cries out from the pit of need. This group of bound prisoners are typical representatives of that large multitude who have fallen into snares and traps and who must suffer until rescued by the divine Redeemer. When Jesus came to Nazareth to preach before his neighbors He turned for His text to the verse in Isaiah: *The Spirit of the Lord is upon me. He hath sent me to proclaim liberty to the captives.* If our Lord could take the figure and apply it to those who are bound by sin's chains surely we may be free to follow Him.

They are represented as prisoners because of rebellion against God's authority. Sin has brought God's wrath upon them. That was literally true of Israel as a nation. The Babylonian captivity came because Israel forgot God, turned away from Him, rebelled against His will for their lives, refused to listen to His messengers, and continued their own willful way toward ruin and bondage and misery.

Godless life brings a bondage that is worse than anything Babylon could devise. Sin's chains are more binding than Nebuchadrezzar could impose. A soul is more utterly helpless under the devil's heel than any man in slavery. These men are represented as helpless and without hope. Every avenue of escape has been tried and found wanting. Despair settles quietly over them.

It is encouraging to know that they were finally driven to prayer. It is always the one and only door. God understands that they are driven to pray as the last expedient. He is ready to hear and rescue them even in this condition. We could wish that needy souls might come to Him before dire necessity drives them to appeal for divine intervention, but this poem is picturing certain instances where men wait until it is almost indecent to appeal for help. We should not lose sight of the thought that true liberty comes when the sinner submits and accepts the proffered salvation. The Saviour works His work of salvation. The chains fall off and the soul is alive again in Him. It is God's merciful way. The psalmist is right in his urgent plea for praise and gratitude. Surely we need to go to Him over and over again with fervent thanks for our own salvation.

THE AFFLICTED ONES (17-22)

To reveal God's goodness the poet gives us another example. Here we see people who have brought upon themselves terrible sickness by their own sinful practices. It is a horrible scene. To what depths men who are created in the image of God can plunge themselves! How vile and hideous and miserable they can become! How helpless they are! How foolish they were in going against all laws of man and God to gratify some urge of their lower natures! We do not wonder at the word "fools" or "foolish ones" that he uses to describe them. Is it not true that all sin is folly? Why do we do it? Why are we so foolish? By foolish sins men drag down their health, destroy the powers of the mind, and ruin the spiritual qualities until sickness is the result. By sin they drag down a full load of grief and suffering and agony upon their own heads.

These men were at the last ditch. Death was standing at the head of the bed ready to take the helpless victims away. Before going the sufferers use what little strength they have to cry out to the one physician who can do anything for sick souls. If the reader is disposed to object because these poor creatures are driven by despair to turn to God let him be reminded again that it is a part of the author's plan to represent four groups in dire peril who in the last moment of life became willing to call upon the Deliverer who is infinitely *good* and who delights to answer any call from anyone.

The answer to that urgent cry thrills our souls. We are told that *He sent His Word and healed them*. The *word* of Jehovah is here personified as a powerful messenger who gladly makes the journey to heal and to restore those so near the end. His messenger does His will (cf. Psalms 105:19, 147:15, 18; Isaiah 55:11; Job 33:23; and John 1:1). Perhaps the psalmist was not able to understand all that was involved in the use of that expression but in the fullness of time Jesus would come to announce Himself as the Incarnate Word (*Logos*) who would be able to heal all manner of sickness and rescue men from the brink of the grave. He would deliver men from sin's power and kill the fatal blood stream infection so that life and not death could be their portion. All of the victories over sickness and death and sin are due to His glorious victory on Calvary and His resurrection from the grave. He is the true Emancipator, our Redeemer and Saviour. Again we are reminded that gratitude impels us to thank Him and to offer sacrifices of thanksgiving to Him. How often do we turn to Him in praise and thanksgiving when He has answered urgent prayers for healing?

THE STORM-TOSSED ONES (23-32)

The fourth example of Jehovah's goodness is the signal deliverance of a group of sailors caught in a mighty storm at sea. The terrors incident to such a storm are vividly pictured. The wind springs up suddenly and dashes with cruel force upon the little ship. The waves respond quickly and take up their destructive role. Noise and dashing water add to the confusion. The unfortunate boat becomes the plaything of the rolling waves. The sailors are frightened out of their wits. No such storm has been seen in all their days. Hope rapidly flies away. How could one hope in such desperate circumstances? What are sailors supposed to do in an emergency like this one? Dr. Sampey used to tell of a storm at sea when passengers were alarmed and kept coming to the captain for assurance. Finally he took one of the pious ladies to the opening leading to the hold of the ship and, pointing to the sailors gambling on the floor below, said, "As long as they continue to gamble you need not worry." Later in the day as she peered over the rail and saw them she was heard to say: "Thank the Lord, they are still at it." It is possible to become frightened to the point where even hardened sailors will pray. Many of us prayed when our brave sons threw themselves in the thick of battle or flew into the teeth of death. Did you ever pray so fervently as in those terrible days and nights?

The men in our psalm were face to face with death and knew it. No steering device or human wisdom could do anything to help them. They turned in humble prayer to God and He heard them above the shriek of the storm. Instantly they were saved and brought safely to their homes where loved ones could enjoy them. It was the poet's way of saying that God is *good* and that man may come to his extremity in disobedience or by accident only to find that He has the divine promise that help is available. God is able. He is available. He will save. He is *good*.

> Jesus, Saviour, pilot me
> Over life's tempestuous sea;
> Unknown waves before me roll,
> Hiding rock and treach'rous shoal;
> Chart and compass come from Thee,
> Jesus, Saviour, pilot me.
>
> As a mother stills her child,
> Thou canst hush the ocean wild;
> Boist'rous waves obey Thy will
> When Thou say'st to them "Be still!"
> Wondrous Sovereign of the sea,
> Jesus, Saviour, pilot me.

What can we say today to multitudes of our people who go carelessly along the way without God and without an anchor that will hold in some tragic hour that is almost certain to come along the way? So many families, concerned only with getting material things, forget God. Many are openly rebellious and make light of a word that reminds them of spiritual needs. Some are concerned and expect to turn to Him one day when the convenient time comes. The psalmist would have us reach all men everywhere with the heartening assurance that our God is a merciful Father who yearns and watches and waits for the return of a wayward prodigal. Even though he should come to himself in a far country with hunger and disease and helplessness driving him to prayer he can confidently expect the Good Shepherd to come instantly to the rescue. It is the way of love. It is the sacrificial love of God that will save unto the uttermost anyone who turns to Him. Our Saviour has revealed depths of love that make us even more eager to take that saving gospel message to lost men everywhere. He **loves.** He died. He lives. He will save.

XVI
A FIXED HEART SINGS

PSALM 57

Be gracious to me, O God, be gracious to me; for my soul trusts
in thee: yea, in the shadow of thy wings will I seek refuge, until
these calamities shall pass by. I will cry to God most high; to
God that performs all things for me. He will send from heaven,
and save me from the reproach of him that would swallow me up.
God will send forth his mercy and his truth. My soul is among
lions; and I lie even among them that breathe out flames, even
the sons of men, whose teeth are spears and arrows, and their
tongue a sharp sword. Be thou exalted, O God, above the heavens;
let thy glory be over all the earth. They have prepared a net for
my steps; my soul is bowed down: they have digged a pit before
me, into the midst of it they have fallen. My heart is fixed, O God,
my heart is fixed; I will sing and give praise. Awake up, my
glory; awake, lute and harp. I myself will awake the dawn. I will
praise thee, O Lord, among the people. I will sing praise to thee
among the nations. For thy mercy is great unto the heavens, and
thy truth unto the clouds. Be thou exalted, O God, above the
heavens: let thy glory be above all the earth.

W OULD you like to examine the faith of a fugitive? Are
you interested to know how he can sing, *my heart is
fixed, O God?* Would you be ready to adopt the method
David used to rise from fear and doubt to the fixity of heart
that issued in a song? We may be sure that this question
reaches and deals with a hunger that is universal. We do
want to be conquerors. We want "a faith that will not shrink"

and a certainty that will give us conquering courage in the midst of foes that may be as deadly as David's foes. A careful study of this psalm will pay large dividends.

The psalmist is in a dangerous spot. Saul and his men are after him in dead earnest. Spies are ready to betray his hiding place at any moment. In an instant sudden death may come to end his career. Wild animals add to the other perils. Every· thing seems to be against him. How can a man hope to write a psalm under such conditions? He did it though and with such beautiful faith and confidence that a part of the psalm has been taken to form the basis of Psalm 108, and the whole message has lived through these thirty centuries as a worthy prayer for any man in distress who needs words to express his inner heart's desire. David began in the depths of something that was closely akin to despair and sang himself into a confident faith that literally breathes hope and courage and serenity of soul.

AN EARNEST PRAYER (1-5)

The psalmist begins with a double cry for mercy, *Be merciful unto me; be merciful unto me, O God!* He is in a desperate predicament and knows that, in his helplessness, he needs the strong arm of God stretched out to snatch him from suffering and death. Quite often it takes tragic circumstances to bring us back to the place where we recognize our inability and our utter dependence upon God. The psalmist was on the road to deliverance and blessings when with proper humility he cried out for divine mercy.

In the midst of danger, with all other avenues of escape cut off, he decides to flee as a helpless little bird to the waiting arms of God. We can hear him saying:

> Jesus, Lover of my soul,
> Let me to Thy bosom fly,
> While the nearer waters roll,
> While the tempest still is high!

> Hide me, O my Saviour, hide,
> Till the storm of life is past;
> Safe into the haven guide,
> O receive my soul at last.

As he becomes conscious of the presence of the eternal Saviour it is natural for him to fly to Him. You have heard of the bird, pursued by a cruel foe, that flew into the very arms of a man and then snuggled up close to his chest for refuge. That is the figure we have here when the psalmist says: *In the shadow of thy wings I will make my refuge until calamities be overpast.* He knows that a helpless soul that trusts has a right to the protecting love of his God. It is the same expression used in the book of Ruth (2:12): *Under whose wings thou hast come to rest.* Our Lord uses the figure (Matthew 23:37) when he says: *How often would I have gathered thy children together, even as a hen gathers her chickens under her wings.* It is good to find an Old Testament saint in the midst of danger giving expression to such a beautiful thought.

In this intimate picture he uses three expressions that give color to his confident trust: *My soul trusteth in thee*, and *in the shadow of thy wings*, and *my refuge*. How tender and childlike is his trust! How precious the imagery! How secure and peaceful the resting place! While man-killing horrors roar about him he is keenly conscious of a quiet calm, a safe retreat, a confident faith that makes his hiding place a palace, securely guarded, entirely surrounded, safely watched, by the eternal Father God. Do you wonder that the fugitive found it in his heart to tell of the marvelous love of his Protector? Even the wild beast that stands by the door of his tent ready to devour him is helpless as God reaches out to deliver His trusting child.

In this prayer David shows a humility that is striking. How we need to learn from him the proper approach to God! He reveals a quiet trust in God that must have been born of experiences that spoke volumes as to God's dependability as well as His availability and willingness to help. The prayer also breathes a spirit of forbearance and patience that declares he is willing to wait for God's own time for the working out of His plan for the kingdom. It could have been otherwise. Saul could have been killed to help God along with His plans. David shows remarkable patience in continuing to wait until the hour of God's own move. His commitment of his body, his personal safety, his future advancement, and his hopes for usefulness, to God's keeping sets him out as a rare creature. He knows quite a bit about God. He is willing to trust everything into His keeping. He knows that the storm that roars overhead will *be overpast*. He is confident of the better day. He is conscious of a steadfast love, of an eternity-long purpose, of an abiding communion of thought with God, of his complete dependence upon God, and of the ultimate triumph of God's plan and purpose. He has confidence in the *Worker* and will leave it all to Him.

In the midst of such fervent praying and such beautiful trust the psalmist suddenly becomes conscious of the enemies again. He is a human being and cannot hope to be completely immune to danger even if he has just professed such a grand trust. These lions are very real and are set to destroy God's anointed. For a brief moment he gives his attention to them but soon turns back to his praying with an earnestness that surpasses his former experience. He gives expression to a strong determination, *I will lie down* to rest among these deadly foes in the consciousness that God will care for His own. It is then that he pours forth the closing line of the prayer (5) in which no personal safety is mentioned. He has settled that and is now interested in the working out of the glory of God. It is his sublime chorus: *Be thou exalted, O God, above the heavens; let thy glory be above all the earth.*

OUTSPOKEN PRAISE (6-11)

The psalmist has been unselfish in his prayer. He now sees (6) the answer to that prayer. God's supreme authority over everything and every person is fully manifested. His foes are seen falling into the very pit they have prepared for him. How better to bring about the triumph of God's cause than for foes to be utterly destroyed in their own pits? David's patience and forbearance and waiting are all vindicated in a way that words cannot describe. God's will is being worked out. His plans must be fulfilled. He will reign over all. The enemies are gone. Praise must take the place of prayer.

He uses the same words in praise that he used in his petition. There is a new quality in his voice, a new joy in his heart. Prayer has a way of changing things. What a difference it would make in our days and in our nights if we prayed it through as thoroughly as our psalmist did! How many eager foes could be defeated and how many fears could be driven away completely if we prayed! Do you know the way to open, full-throated praise? Try the kind of prayer David has just revealed to us. It has been and will always be the way to victory, to faith, and to praise. Instead of sleepless nights, heavy crosses, frightening fears, why not *steal away to Jesus*, and, as a frightened bird, pillow your head on the divine bosom? Let the encircling arms of the eternal Keeper bring peace to your soul.

David found stability through persevering prayer. Instantly he breaks out into a grand burst of praise, *my heart is fixed, O God, my heart is fixed, I will sing and give praise.* He knows that he has an anchor. He can feel the pull. He has difficulty finding words to carry the rapture of a delivered soul which owes everything to God. He realizes that he is in the midst of a world of storms and torrents. He has had his fluttering, wandering heart lashed down to the solid rock from which no tempest can blow him. Anchored to God the heart is firm. He is rooted, anchored, lashed to, securely fastened to his God who is the solid Rock of Ages. In Him he will find every need provided so that his whole life can be devoted to the cause of bringing glory to that *Name that is above every name*. He is *kept by the power of God*. He will keep on keeping as His child keeps on trusting.

Such fixity of heart calls for a song. Even though the night is dark he is sure morning will come. He utters a rather bold saying when he declares that he will *wake the dawn* with his song. Before the break of day he will go forth shouting the praises of his dear Lord who has brought about this superb faith in his soul. The kind of mercy and the kind of truth that have met in Him call for world-wide praise from the hearts and throats of redeemed individuals.

How may we learn the secret? Is it possible for us to find simple trust, courage, confidence, and that quality of soul expressed in our text, *my heart is fixed, O God*? Let us hope that it will not be necessary for us to suffer as David suffered nor to be frightened by cruel foes as he was forced to face. We may rest assured though that such experiences prepare the way for the clearest and fullest faith. Adversity, disappointment, pain, sorrow, distress, may be necessary in many instances. At any rate such experiences tend to drive a man back to God and reveal something of the weakness of human ability in tragic hours. David learned his lessons the hard way. Some of us will follow in his train.

We must come to the place where human strength is found to be inadequate and where the soul is willing to turn to God for His guiding hand in learning the way to power and to victory. Having learned this we must pray for cleansing and for forgiveness so that we can come into that sacred place with the holy God. How often we could count on a rich blessing for our hearts if we were not out of tune with God and unfit to stand in His presence! When we recognize our need and realize that we can do nothing about it for ourselves and understand that God is able to make victory possible we are led to earnest prayer. How poor we are because we do not pray! How puny and weak and helpless we are because we do not ask Him for His answer! David gives us an example of importunate prayer that holds on until the divine answer comes. We can see the response even while he continues in prayer. We can have victories when we pray.

You recall the dramatic story in the sixth chapter of II Kings that tells of the fears of Elisha's servant when he saw such a multitude surrounding the little city. No avenue of escape could be found. Capture and death loomed as inevitable. Syrians were cruel. What could be done? The young man ran to the great prophet with the question: *Master, how shall we do?* Elisha closed his eyes in prayer. We may be sure the servant was surprised that no prayer was offered for deliverance from their desperate plight but that he said: *Lord, open his eyes that he may see.* What a strange prayer for such an emergency! We are told that his eyes were opened and he saw a multitude of horses and chariots of fire round about the entire city. Eternal protection was available. He learned that *they that be for us are more than they that be against us.* What courage such an understanding gives! In the midst of all the foes and dangers and hostile men one can be calm and courageous and steadfast. How we need this strong assurance in our day!

Jesus had a way of appearing in the hour of distress and peril and fear with the words, *fear not.* In the Greek literally He is saying: *quit fearing.* He wanted desperately to quiet fears, to restore calm confidence, to give hope and courage and serenity. No life is happy or effective when fear has its grip on the mind. Paralysis renders one strangely ineffective. Jesus said: *I am come that ye may have life and that ye may have it more abundantly*. Surely this is the thing He was including in that statement. In His closing words to His disciples he said: *Lo, I am with you always*. That line gives us a golden assurance for all our days. In the bearing of burdens He will be with us. No matter how heavy the load His presence will make the journey possible. When strength is almost gone He gives the needed supply from this reservoir. Burdens can be borne as He holds us. In meeting the tempter He supplies the necessary power to make victory possible. We can say with Paul: *We are therefore more than conquerors through Him that loves us*. In conquering fears no other antidote can possibly be found to compare with the thrilling realization that He is in the room with us. Fears fly out the window when we realize that He is by our side. In hours of loneliness and despair we can be cheered and lifted by the consciousness that our Elder Brother who became our Saviour is by our side. What raptures of delight fill our soul when we come to know of His presence! How much lighter the road! How joyous the heart! How marvelous the way!

David was giving utterance to something of the essence of the New Testament doctrine when he wrote this psalm. He had found a wondrous secret. That secret was working in his heart and in his experience. Serenity of soul had become his possession. The bells were ringing in his soul. A strong certainty gripped him. He was ready to meet hostile foes, climb steep heights, engage in hard climbs, work unceasingly for His God, in the consciousness that he was equipped to be one of God's earthly representatives. His Deliverer was depending on him. Surely we have more ground for confidence and courage, more reason for joy and thanksgiving, more cause for wholehearted commitment of life and talents, and more reason to become a witness of all His matchless grace to men. May His Spirit lead us to say,

Lead on, O King Eternal!
The day of march has come;
Henceforth in fields of conquest
Thy tents shall be our home.
Thro' days of preparation,
Thy grace has made us strong,
And now, O King Eternal,
We lift our battle song.

Lead on, O King Eternal!
We follow, not with fears;
For gladness breaks like morning
Where'er Thy face appears;
Thy cross is lifted o'er us;
We journey in its light:
The crown awaits the conquest;
Lead on, O God of might.

XVII

OLD HUNDRED

PSALM 100

Make a joyful noise unto the Lord, all ye lands. Serve the Lord with gladness: come before his presence with singing. Know ye that the Lord he is God: it is he that has made us, and not we ourselves; we are his people, and the sheep of his pasture. Enter into his gates with thanksgiving, and into his courts with praise. Give thanks to him. For the Lord is good; his mercy is everlasting; and his truth endures to all generations.

Praise God from whom all blessings flow;
Praise Him all creatures here below;
Praise Him above, ye heavenly host;
Praise Father, Son, and Holy Ghost.

No four lines in all English poetry are more familiar or more generally used than these immortal lines from the pen of Thomas Ken. He merely adapted the lofty thoughts of Psalm 100 and gave it to minds and hearts that respond to the strange appeal. Jews and Christians unite in using, enjoying, and remembering the message of this brief poem. No psalm is used more frequently in synagogue or in church. It is God's word to the inner heart of man calling for praise and thanksgiving and joyous service. There is not one single mournful note in the entire psalm. The psalmist praises

God from beginning to end and calls on the earth to join
with him in praise and thanksgiving and adoration. He
is so happy that he must have others join him in the
praises.

William Kethe in 1561 gave us the beautiful paraphrase
that has entered into the thought and literature of the outstanding poets and scholars of the world. His poem is as
follows:

> All people that on earth do dwell,
> Sing to the Lord with cheerful voice;
> Him serve with fear,
> His praise forth tell;
> Come before Him and rejoice.
> Know that the Lord is God indeed;
> Without our aid He did us make;
> We are His flock, He doth us feed,
> And for His sheep He doth us take.

Shout Unto the Lord (1; cf. 98:4, 95:1, 2)

The theme of the poem is expressed in this first line
usually translated, *make a joyful noise unto the Lord*. The
figure is that of a crowd of loyal subjects expressing their
awakened emotions as their king suddenly appears. The air
is filled with noisy shouts of praise and adoration as the
king walks before them. Our God inspires happy, cheerful
worship. Those who are fortunate enough to be in His
presence are stirred by the inner urge to break forth into
singing and jubilant praise. In acclaiming Him as their
King the subjects are moved to express themselves in a loud
and joyous manner. The psalmist crosses all racial barriers
and urges all peoples of the earth to join with him in this
glad acclaim to the King of the whole earth. He is worthy.
He is the Creator and Preserver. He is the Guide and Keeper.

He is the One to whom all may look for the blessings each heart needs. He loves and plans for and watches over the ones He has created.

Serve the Lord with Gladness

Gladsome worship will eventuate in happy service. The ones who welcome their King with shouts of joy and praise will be the happiest as they dedicate their talents, their time, their whole beings to the fullest service. They are the ones who really enjoy their grip on God. There is no bondage or toil or slavery there. There is plenty of work and plenty of obedience but the dominant note is the note of jubilant joy. Even the Lord enjoys having His creatures around Him because they are happy in the consciousness that they are near Him and busy about His business.

How is it in your church, in your home, in your community? Does God detect a note of joy in your countenance, in your words, in your service? Far too few of us are genuinely happy. We give a definite impression of being sad or miserable or pessimistic. Our faces are not radiant, our eyes have too little light in them, our words carry altogether too little of the lift for other hearts that may be sad. We are so anxious that our church services may be dignified and according to the ritual, that we squeeze out practically all the spirit of thanksgiving and rejoicing. Even the songs may lack the note of happiness or rejoicing. Do we really praise Him? Can a young person or a stranger hear the strains of the joybells? Look carefully at the faces of the minister, the members of the choir, the organist, the one who makes the announcements, the ones who take the offering, and then look about through the congregation to see how much real joy you can find. Is it any wonder that the little boy whispered in his mother's ear: "Is God dead?"

This psalmist is writing to individuals who needed to

light up their faces by an inner experience of gratitude and rejoicing. Why not be radiantly happy? Why should we be so selfish and self-centered that we stifle every breath of praise before it is half grown? We who have been redeemed by the blood of Christ and have Him constantly in our hearts and lives have more cause for rejoicing and singing than all the Old Testament saints put together. Why not sing?

> He lives, He lives, Christ Jesus lives today!
> He walks with me and talks with me
> Along life's narrow way.
> He lives, He lives, salvation to impart!
> You ask me how I know He lives?
> He lives within my heart.[1]

KNOW THAT THE LORD IS GOD

The heart cries out for certainty. Minds grope and search for the kind of evidence that will stand in the hour of testing. This verse exhorts us to know for a certainty that Jehovah is God. How certain are you of this fact? Is he the eternal God of all the universe with unlimited power, with absolute knowledge, with the ability to be present everywhere to speak to the heart of one of His creatures? With awe and reverence we will bow before Him and worship Him and rejoice in the thought that He is our God. *It is He that hath made us, and not we ourselves; we are his people, and the sheep of his pasture.* Jehovah is the Creator of the world and of His creatures. He made Israel to be His special, chosen people and gave to them the personal care that prepared them to be a light to the peoples of the earth. Even though they have sinned He has not disowned them. They may still claim Him as their Shepherd and Guide. They still belong to Him.

As Creator He has special rights and claims. He made us for Himself that He might have creatures on whom He could lavish His love and who would love Him with a true affection. No one can claim any ownership rights in us and no other master has any reason to expect us to be loyal to him nor to pay homage to him. Jehovah is our rightful owner and the one who may hold the reins and carry the keys to our heart. One of the readings of the Hebrew text is to be translated "and we are His." Since this is true He is our Sovereign Ruler. Glad-hearted devotion to Him as the absolute Lord of our life will bring joy to Him and cultivate a rare grace in our own hearts. He is our Protector and Guide and Shepherd. Infinite patience and care and love enter into the daily ministries that make our lives rich and full. We take it for granted that we are largely responsible for the comforts and luxuries and necessities that make our lives happy. If we could see the hand of our Shepherd gently placing love tokens in reach of our greedy hands we would be more apt to respond as our author asks of us in the opening verses of this psalm.

He has a right to our best love, our fullest gratitude, our fervent praise, and our most devoted service because: (1) He created us. The Creator always has full control over the creature. He is fully responsible for bringing the creature into being. Surely no one would dispute God's right to control and use the work of His hands to the last limit of His desire. (2) He has redeemed us from bondage and slavery. No right is stronger than the right of one who has paid the ransom price and bought back the slave from the one who owned him. Those of us who recognize the atoning work of Christ can but bow in grateful acknowledgment of His right to control and to direct our lives for we are truly His slaves. (3) His marvelous love for us claims the best love, the truest devotion, and the utmost in service. No stronger cord can ever bind us than the cords of love so clearly seen as we look upon the incarnation, the life, and the death of our Lord and Saviour. He has demonstrated a love that was willing to give all to redeem a vile sinner. (4) His purpose for our lives. When we are taken into the secret place and allowed to see the divine blueprints for our lives we are swept with a deep longing to measure up to the purpose He has for our lives. If He expects so much of us surely we will exert every energy to help fulfill His plan and purpose. (5) His provisions for our happiness at the end of the journey. Just one glimpse at the home prepared for us on the other shore should call forth the breaking up of the deep wells of gratitude so that an overflowing stream of thanksgiving will pour out to gladden the heart of God. In the light of all this any one of us can break forth into joyous singing and let all the people around us know that we are desperately in love with our Lord and King. Genuine praise from grateful hearts will be the most natural response. Who can withhold full-throated praise when such evidences are presented?

ENTER INTO HIS GATES WITH THANKSGIVING (4)

The one who thinks will thank. These two words are closely related. When we enter His holy place we will experience a wave of genuine gratitude that expresses itself in thanksgiving. The most normal response is the expression of thanks to our Father God who has done so much for us. Our minds are flooded with the reality of so many gifts and blessings and good things that we are humbled before Him and our hearts pour forth thanks and praise. When we go into the sanctuary we are brought face to face with God and we will bless His name. How we need the true worship service where the individuals are led to listen for God's voice and respond as joyful worshipers in praise and thanksgiving. Do we provide the proper atmosphere for man to find God and to commune with Him? Are we making men conscious of the presence of God? Is worship the dominant note in our meetings? Do we lead the way for the people to praise and to sing and to thank and to worship? A full appreciation of the meaning and message of this psalm will help tremendously. We cannot live selfish, godless lives when we pause to think of His love for us and of His longing to have us come into His sanctuary for worship and praise.

Jehovah Is Good. His Mercy Is Everlasting (5)

In this brief line a grand summary is given that reminds us again of His love and mercy and faithfulness. Being gracious, kind, bountiful, and loving His creatures can depend on Him to continue always as a helpful Friend who seeks for opportunities to bring blessings into their lives. Such mercy is the occasion for the highest praise. No one who looks upon the unlimited mercy of God can be silent before Him. Unrestrained praise and thanksgiving will be evident all through the day and throughout his entire life. Jehovah's goodness calls forth a response that makes the portals of heaven ring with joyful praise. We will be happier. Our friends and neighbors will be constrained to worship Him and God's heart will rejoice.

In our day when strain and confusion and disturbing crises claim our attention and keep the radiance from our faces and souls it is good to have a psalm that has been sung across so many ages and has sustained so many pilgrims. Even in the darkest hours of history, voices have blended in singing this anthem of praise. The religious joy depicted here is not just "a bubbling emotion or frothy sentiment" dependent upon sunshine and prosperity and peace and apt to disappear when suffering or adversity or calamity come into the life. No storm or cloud or calamity can drive it from the soul because it can say: *The Lord is God; it is He that hath made us, and not we ourselves, we are His people, and the sheep of His pasture.* The triumphant trust displayed in its lines is sorely needed among our people today. In the midst of tragedy, in the face of perils, in the hour of sorrow, may we anchor our faith in the Rock of Ages and turn our hearts and voices heavenward in prayer and praise and thanksgiving.

Remembering that we are His people, and the sheep of His pasture, we can think of His unfailing guidance, His loving care, and His eternal provisions for our blessedness. Surely such contemplations will lift our hearts in the kind of praise that will delight His heart and make His days happier as He rejoices in His creatures.

Enter into His gates with thanksgiving and into His courts with praise.

XVIII

A THIRST FOR THE
LIVING GOD

PSALMS 42 and 43

As the hart panteth after the water brooks, so panteth my soul
after thee, O God. My soul thirsteth for God, for the living God.
When shall I come and appear before God? My tears have been
my meat day and night, while they continually say unto me,
Where is thy God? When I remember these things, I pour out my
soul in me, for I had gone with the multitude, I went with them
to the house of God, with the voice of joy and praise, with a
multitude that kept holyday. Why art thou cast down, O my soul?
Why art thou disquieted in me? Hope thou in God, for I shall yet
praise him. . . .

My soul is cast down within me: therefore will I remember. . . .
Deep calleth unto deep at the noise of thy waterspouts. All thy
waves and thy billows have gone over me. Yet the Lord will command his loving-kindness in the daytime, and in the night his
song shall be with me, and my prayer unto the God of my life.
. . . Why go I mourning because of the oppression of the enemy?
. . . Mine enemies reproach me; while they say daily unto me,
Where is thy God? Why art thou cast down, O my soul? and why
art thou disquieted within me? Hope thou in God, for I shall
yet praise him. . . .

Judge me, O God, and plead my cause against an ungodly
nation. . . . For thou art the God of my strength. Why dost thou
cast me off? Why go I mourning because of the oppression of the
enemy? O send out thy light and thy truth; let them lead me; let
them bring me to thy holy hill. . . . Then will I go unto the

altar of God, unto God my exceeding joy: yea, upon the harp will I praise thee, O God my God. Why art thou cast down, O my soul? Why art thou disquieted within me? Hope in God, for I shall yet praise him.

WHAT is more pathetic than a person or beast literally dying of thirst? In our land it is next to impossible for one to realize the tragic situation. The author of our psalm lived in the country where water is scarce and where thirst is better known. He is thinking of a pathetic scene by a dry water course. A famished hind has made the long journey only to find a dry hole. In desperation she searches everywhere for a bit of water to relieve her thirst only to be mocked by hot, unsatisfying sand. Not even a moist place in the sand can be found. She is without hope. Nothing can satisfy her. Every spring has dried up. She can only dream of better days when sparkling water supplied all her needs and refreshed her for hard journeys. The psalmist recognizes a picture of himself. He is in enemy territory. Nothing in all that area provides the help his thirsty soul craves. He longs for the presence of God in His sanctuary. A devastating wave of loneliness overwhelms him. Enemies mock and taunt him. A sickening doubt creeps into his mind. He is on the very verge of the tragic disease brought on by losing God. He must have his thirst satisfied. How can he find God's presence? Tears have been his food day and night. He turns in faith to the One who can supply all needs and refresh with full satisfaction. He says: *My soul thirsts for God, for the living God; when shall I come to appear before God?*

Without question the poem making up Psalms 42 and 43 is a single composition. The same theme is presented, the same style and language are apparent, the same spirit is seen, the same refrain recurs at regular intervals. No title is affixed to Psalm 43. It seems almost certain that they were originally one although the separation is quite old since the Septuagint has them separate. There are three main divisions, each ending in the familiar refrain. 1-5: A thirsty soul cries out for God in the midst of sorrows and insults. 6-11: A description of his pitiable plight and his determination to pray to his listening God. 1-3: An earnest prayer for deliverance and full restoration. He begs for communion with God. What greater boon can any soul ask? Who can seek for a higher blessing? It will be a sublime discovery when we as twentieth century Christians come to understand the full treasure thus described and turn in eager search for that satisfaction.

We cannot know much about the author except the unforgettable picture which he paints of himself. He is one of the descendants of Korah. These men usually gave themselves to serving about the Temple. This poet had been an active member of this group and had taken his place at the head of bands of pilgrims as they walked in holy processions about the Temple. Now he is denied this privilege. In some way he is kept in exile in the country near Mount Hermon. Instead of happy voices shouting praise to Jehovah he hears raucous voices heaping ridicule and insult upon him as ungodly pagans taunt him about the failure of his God (Jehovah) to protect, to keep, and to bless him. It is a black hour for him. Out of the depths he cries to his God.

My Soul Thirsts for God

The psalmist is almost certainly suffering from some human ailment that makes him a loathsome object, visible to men who can taunt him with the hastily conceived conclusion that his God has forgotten him. He is not bed-ridden but goes about before his neighbors as a walking picture of one deserted and abandoned by his God. They may look on him as incurable but he still has hope. His God will not leave him to die in this hostile land. Jehovah will come to lift, to heal, and to restore. All of these sufferings are hard to bear but his poignant pain is an intense longing to have fellowship with God. He does not know that God is able to provide the blessings even in a strange land. He seems to be laboring under the impression that worship apart from the sanctuary, the priest, the burnt offerings, and the temple ritual is impossible.

Within his heart is a consuming passion to have God, to feel God, to be blessed by His presence. Suddenly he remembers the good old days when he was a part of the happy throng and had vital touch with God. He knows what it is like. He knows what God does for a soul. He knows how shallow and empty and unsatisfying a life can be when God is not present to bless, to lift, and to supply water to quench thirst. He knows what the touch of His presence means in the life. Would that our own backsliders who once knew the joys of divine blessings might get awake to the empty bit of existence that they now know. Let us help the poet drive these truths home to their thirsty hearts.

Do you know what it is to thirst for God? Is it a universal thirst? Do men and women thirst for Him without understanding the nature of that inner longing? How about the prodigal son or the woman at the well? Outwardly they seemed to be free from any such desire. We may be sure, however, that neither of them had lost the memory of sweeter, richer, fuller days. Each of them looked forward to some satisfying realization of the soul's wish. Each was acutely conscious of the emptiness of life as it was being lived. Memories sometime bring hope. The prodigal had hungers that mere husks could never satisfy. The woman knew of a life that brought rich joys and wholesome dividends. Jesus was able to interpret the meaning of that suppressed ideal. He was able to lead her to reach out a soiled hand for treasures too rich to evaluate. He said: *If you knew the gift of God, and who it is that says to you, give me to drink, you would have asked of him, and he would have given you living water.* It did not take long to bring to her the salvation, the cleansing, the forgiveness, that she so sorely needed. She began to live again. Christ supplied the soul-enriching gift that made life different for her, and through her to the people of her village.

Isaiah gave us that beautiful line: *Ho, every one that thirsteth, come ye to the waters, and he that hath no money; come ye, buy, and eat; yea, come, buy wine and milk without money and without price. Wherefore do ye spend money for that which is not bread? and your labor for that which satisfieth not? Hearken diligently unto me, and eat ye that which is good, and let your soul delight itself in fatness.* It is just like our loving Father to seek to relieve all honest thirst. How marvelous is His love! How tender is His solicitude! The soul that *thirsts for the living God* can be sure of finding the fullest enjoyment of heaven's best remedy. When He comes as the *living* God we know His love as the living love and His will as the living will. A mighty faith takes hold of us and makes victory certain. He gives us the power to walk with Him in faith and to abide in Him even though the body may be in captivity. Who can say that John Bunyan failed to live victoriously even though the walls of Bedford jail closed about him? Paul could say: *We are therefore more than conquerors through Him that loves us.*

Mary Magdalene was living a meaningless existence, bored with shallow rounds of worthless pursuits, until Jesus came. She was not conscious of the tragedy and thirst and hunger of her soul. Jesus awakened a holy desire to commit her body and mind and soul to the Master. Life was different. She began to live. When the newly-risen Lord stood in the bright sunlight of the first Easter morn He gave to Mary Magdalene the precious privilege of going as the first herald of the resurrection.

I heard the voice of Jesus say, "Come unto Me and rest;
Lay down, thou weary one, lay down Thy head upon My breast."
I came to Jesus as I was, weary and worn and sad;
I found in Him a resting place, and He has made me glad.

I heard the voice of Jesus say, "Behold, I freely give
The living water; thirsty one, stoop down, and drink, and live!"
I came to Jesus, and I drank of that life-giving stream;
My thirst was quenched, my soul revived, and now I live in Him.

Dr. Chappell tells the story of the hatching of a strange, ugly creature along with a dozen or more chickens. This awkward bird was never happy in the barnyard. He did not fit in with the chickens. He could not describe his hunger but it was there all the time. One day he heard a wild scream above him and saw an eagle flying swiftly and majestically through the air. In a moment he caught the spark and took off in pursuit of his distant cousin. He was not made for a barnyard and for simple chickens. He was built for speed, for crags, for high mountains, for rare air. No satisfaction could come to him apart from the full realization of that for which he was born. Since we are meant for God, nothing short of fellowship with Him will ever satisfy our poor souls. The unfortunate man in the upper Jordan territory could find no possible joy apart from the presence of his God. Lesser blessings could help but only in Jehovah would he find his soul's desire.

WHERE IS THY GOD?

The pathetic side to the picture is the helpless man before the accusations of the neighbors. He hears them say, *Where is your God?* and is unable to say a word that will silence them or satisfy his own sinking heart. Where is his God? Why is He allowing such suffering? Why does He not come to his rescue? Where is He? Is He weak or busy or uninterested? Has He forgotten? When will He break His silence and come to find His suffering servant? The living present seems to contradict the faith he professed. Missionaries tell us that one of the bitterest pains they are called on to bear is the proud scorn of one who looks on and shows his contempt for the God they claim as a Friend and Deliverer when circumstances seem to prove that He is either asleep or that He has forgotten them. In our own land we may cringe before that question (uttered or unexpressed) as it comes from the secularist, the agnostic, the rationalist, the materialist, the cynic, or the agonizing friend whose faith is about to break under the strain. *Where is thy God?* Can you answer that challenging question? Are you able to convince yourself that He is present and able and interested and kind and that He will help? Would it frighten you to find that you have no answer?

What about that question as it hits you squarely in your complacency and ease and self-satisfied life? *Where is thy God?* In your thoughts, your imaginations, your daydreams, your anxieties, your life ambitions, your plans, your busy schedule, in your activities, your work, your play, your social engagements? Would it be alarming to look up and to see Him?

What is the answer? How does the psalmist answer? We have seen that he does not have a direct answer to the unsympathetic foes. He can but weep and suffer and long for a visit from his divine Friend. In a very real and powerful way he gives forth his answer. He says: *I remember.* What a·flood of glory comes out of that concept! Memory does so much for us. Do you have grand memories that pour in to reveal treasures that no man can take away? The psalmist is transported from the drab, miserable, hopeless situation into a world where shouts and glad music and crowding worshipers hold the center of the stage. He remembers the godly souls who walked the sacred courts, the lavish offerings, the fervent prayers, the sense of the divine presence and the thrill of divine forgiveness. Nothing could steal these sublime realities from his possession. They are real. They bring satisfaction. They remind him of the reality of the God of the ages who is working out His own eternal purpose in and through individuals. *He will not fail. He will not be discouraged. He will* make a glorious *victory* possible. Hope springs up within his soul as he remembers God. Instantly he says: *Why are you bowed down, O my soul, and why do you murmur within me? Hope in God, for I shall yet praise Him.* This refrain is to recur after each stanza to sound the dominant note of the poem. This new hope expresses a definite expectation of higher and richer and better things as God works out His own good purpose. It is God alone who can help. The poet wants God. He will continue to urge his soul to trust, to wait, and to hope. He will grow more confident as the psalm unfolds.

Suppose the poet should turn the question upon his cruel mockers, saying, "Where is *thy God*?" In what do you trust? Did you make him or did he make you? Where is he? What is he doing? How does he help? To what goal is he leading you? What can he do for you in the last hour? It will not be enough to close with that question. The psalmist is perhaps God's one representative in that whole land. It is his place and his privilege to reveal so much of his own great

God that even his mockers will be constrained to learn of Him and to submit to Him. In short the stranger in a strange land can silence the unworthy mockery by giving a demonstration of Christian graces that reveal the true grace of God to men who otherwise never know Him.

AN AGONIZING PRAYER

The thirst finally drives the sufferer to pray to his God. It is the way to victory. He believes that He will answer the insistent question. He calls for the certain proof of concern and love. If He cares He will come to the rescue of the frantic exile. The poet is willing to put his case in God's hands. Trouble has come in cataracts and billows and woes but they are all the creations of God's hand. These troubles but lead him to God. How do you react to trouble, to distress, and to disappointment? Do they drive you to your knees in humble prayer? Are you brought to still your heart so that you can hear God's voice and understand His divine purpose? When you suffer do you let Him draw you close to His own great heart? It is in the dark hour that He is able to reveal His sweetest music and His clearest guidance. It is in that experience that He can set the bells going in your heart.

The psalmist turns in earnest to the One who can provide a just settlement of his problem. Passionately he expresses the deep desires of his heart. He is utterly dependent upon God. He has a strong hope that his prayer will be answered. Light and truth, like guiding angels, will bring him home to God's house. The holy altar will again satisfy the deep longings of his hungry soul. How sweet it is to find hope and confidence and courage returning.

Even though he prays he has not won a complete victory. Fears still plague him, enemies continue to taunt him, uncertainties loom before his mind. Prayer does its work though and the eternal One who answers prayer supplies the source of strength and faith that saves him from doubt and despair and defeat. The whole song is the picture of a soul climbing from the depths to the heights. Often he slips back and loses the precious gains he has just won but he is up and at it all over again to reach new heights and to record new victories. What he really wants is to be found only in *the living God*. No dead thing nor vain abstraction can supply the basic needs of his soul. Even in his darker moments he refuses to let self-pity gain control. He knows that he can count on the living God to keep His promise.

I heard the voice of Jesus say, "I am this dark world's Light: Look unto Me; thy morn shall rise, and all thy day be bright." I looked to Jesus and I found in Him my Star, my Sun; And in that light of life I'll walk till all my journey's done.

Hope and Rejoicing Come

In the first stanza we had gloom and darkness. In the second stanza we saw the conflict of opposite emotions. In this last stanza hope breaks forth as the gift of One who has been listening and is now ready to prove his loving interest by supplying the needs of a praying soul. He is willing to nestle even closer to the One who has revealed Himself as the eternal Keeper on whom trusting souls may lean. It is a great discovery. The enemies are still present. They will continue to insult him. Conditions have not changed. He has changed radically since he has found God. Music will now find a place in his life. Gratitude will well up and overflow in grateful praise. A new day has dawned for him. Faith has had a hard struggle with fear and doubt but she has won a signal victory. Faith will be stronger and clearer and more securely anchored because of the terrific struggle. The psalmist can rejoice in the midst of horrible surroundings because his thirst has been quenched and his grip on God made more certain. He forbids his soul to despair. The shining way to God is seen. *Hope thou in God, for I shall yet praise Him*. He has seen the face of God in the dense darkness. From the black night he has sung himself into peace and confidence and sublime hope. He has obtained *a garland for ashes, a garment of praise for the spirit of heaviness* (Isaiah 61:3). He knows that his prayer is to be answered. God will continue to hear and to answer and to pour out needed blessings. One can almost hear the plaintive plea of Jeremiah rising into triumphant faith because an inner experience with a friendly God. The prayer seems to contain a picture of the inner soul sharing in the climb toward certainty. The heart is slowly but surely brought out of stormy unrest, out of soul agony to a strange stillness that climbs into indescribable joy.

Can God hear the anguished cry of a man today and will He take time to deal with him and lead him through storm and stress and deep darkness into rest and peace and serenity? Can we assure ourselves of His willingness to hear and to bless? Listen to our Lord who said: *If any man thirst, let him come to me and drink*. There is no exception. He is able to respond to every thirst and every cry. *He that cometh to me shall never hunger; and he that believeth on me shall never thirst . . . whosoever drinketh of the water that I shall give him shall never thirst; but the water that I shall give him shall be in him a well of water springing up into everlasting life*. Millions have cried out unto Him and have found these claims to be true. They have tasted and found refreshing streams abundantly able to quench all their thirsts. He alone can satisfy. He gives the healing, the lifting, the transforming touch. He satisfies fully. Let Him come to prove His love and His power to save.

XIX

A MIGHTY FORTRESS

PSALM 46

God is our refuge and strength, a very present help in trouble.
Therefore we will not fear, though the earth be removed, and
though the mountains be carried into the midst of the sea; though
the waters thereof roar and be troubled, though the mountains
shake with the swelling thereof. There is a river whose
streams make glad the city of God, the holy place of the taber-
nacles of the Most High. God is in the midst of her; she shall
not be moved. God will help her, and that right early. The nations
raged, the kingdoms were moved; he uttered his voice, the earth
melted. The Lord of hosts is with us; the God of Jacob is our
refuge. Come, behold the works of the Lord, what desolations he
has made in the earth. He makes wars to cease to the end of the
earth; he breaks the bow, and cuts the spear asunder; he burns
the chariot in the fire. Be still, and know that I am God. I will
be exalted among the nations, I will be exalted in the earth. The
Lord of Hosts is with us; the God of Jacob is our refuge.

WHO has not been moved by the stately "battle song of
the reformation," *Ein feste Burg ist unser Gott?* It has
in it the essence of true patriotic fervor and a strange quality
that stirs confidence and hope and daring. Luther caught up
in that hymn the meaning and message of this psalm. It had
inspired him with courage to defy the pope and the whole
system of ecclesiastical tyranny. In it he visualized the eternal
God who could bring about His own will even though a

multitude of foes sought to have their way. All these rebellious beings were utterly helpless before the mighty arm of *the Lord of Hosts*. His faith is stronger with each singing of the challenging lines. Staerk says: "It is the most glorious hymn of faith that ever was sung." Kittel says: "If we can call I Corinthians 13 the Hohelied of Love, we can with the same right call this Psalm the Hohelied of Faith."

Oliver Cromwell, seeking to make England an emblem of heaven where God's will reigns supreme, asked his people to sing Luther's great hymn. "That," he says, "is a rare psalm for a Christian. *God is our refuge and strength, a very present help in trouble.* If pope and Spaniard and devil set themselves against us, yet in the name of the Lord we shall destroy them. *The Lord of Hosts is with us, the God of Jacob is our refuge.*" As the great John Wesley lay dying in London many thoughts clamored for utterance. His closing words were: *The Lord of Hosts is with us, the God of Jacob is our refuge.*

As early as the fourteenth century this psalm exerted a profound influence upon Christians. Sergius, the hermit, used it in rousing his countrymen when Tartar hordes were running over the entire land. Over and over the godly hermit recited Psalm 46 and then led the revived men in a charge that drove the invaders back and guaranteed victory. All through the ages men have been stirred by the realization that the eternal God is available with sufficient power to do anything. Earthquakes, disasters, invasions, desperate situations, need not overwhelm one who realizes the presence of *Jehovah of Hosts* who controls everything and everybody at all times and in all places. When we stop to think it through, we are not surprised that men of all ages and all lands have found in this poem the basis for confidence and hope and certainty. No foe is too strong, no disaster too deadly, no danger too much for one who grips the firm hand of the eternal God. It is a psalm of triumph. *The Lord of Hosts is with us, the God of Jacob is our refuge.* Born in the hour of gloom and danger and defeat, it has proved to be a victory tonic as men have risen to march to the heights, guided and sustained by His strong hand.

In the midst of dark days the poet spoke these heartening words. Fear and dread covered the people like a blanket. Sennacherib and his invincible army had driven across Palestine without anything that resembled opposition. Egypt had been found wanting as an ally. Hezekiah and his trembling people huddled helplessly behind the walls of Jerusalem. Assyrian battering rams would soon break down the walls and God's holy city would be no more. If Phoenicians, Philistines and Egyptians were powerless before him how could the puny army of Judah hope to offer even feeble resistance? Who would be foolish enough to have hope in his heart in such an evil day? In the darkest day Isaiah, the prophet, came forth with the assurance that Jerusalem was safe and that not an arrow would fall within the city. He made it clear that such precious security was not the result of arms and men but because of the presence of *Jehovah of Hosts.* He had decreed that His city would be safe. We know the facts of the spectacular deliverance of Jerusalem when Sennacherib lost one hundred and eighty-five thousand men and was forced to flee to his home in Assyria.

Our psalm seems to have been born in that dramatic experience. Hope lives again. Despair and gloom and fear have all been driven away. God has demonstrated His love, His power, His willingness to save His own in the hour of distress. In the light of this signal deliverance the author has a tremendous faith in God and wants to instill something of that same trust in the hearts of his people. He knows that God is dependable. He knows that He is available. He knows that dark hours give Him the opportunity to demonstrate all these attributes. He has put the trumpet to his lips that men of all ages might have built for them the basis for a mighty faith.

THE OUTLINE

The psalm has three distinct divisions each with four verses (if we agree that originally the refrain followed verse three as it does verses six and ten). In verses one to three we have a challenge to confidence that looks upward to God who is the refuge of His people. In verses four to seven we see the secret of that confidence as our eyes are turned upon the signal display of God's power and mercy in the recent deliverance. In verses eight to eleven we have an outward look that tells of the vindication of that confidence and declares that God can be depended upon to bring about His final supremacy over all nations. He is the sovereign God.

CONFIDENCE IN GOD (1-3)

It is good to have faith in God. What would we do without it? How could we bear up in tragic hours of disappointment and sorrow and loss and despair? The first word is *God*. Why fear anything or anyone if we have God? He sees God as a *Refuge* in whom we can hide from the storm; the *Strength* to guarantee stability; the *Help*, present every moment to lift and hearten and save. Everything man has claimed as a foundation is on the point of crumbling. Even the mountains are toppling over into the swirling waters to find the old resting place used before God had completed His creation. The ocean sweeps relentlessly on over hill and city and valley with certain destruction for everyone in its path. Death and disaster loom for every creature. In addition to natural visitations a horde of fiendish invaders swarms over the land. Fear comes swiftly to take up residence in every heart. Who can keep fear out? Hope is dead. Dread is on the throne. In the midst of danger and despair the poet finds the solution. God is there! He is the high tower into which every fear-stricken man may climb for protection and solace and comfort and safety. No mountain or raging sea can touch him there. He is safe from every harm. *Let the waters rage and foam. . . . Let the mountain quake at the proud swelling thereof.* What of it? Those who have the eternal God for refuge in such a storm have the basis for calm confidence and unbounding joy. He is not only a sure refuge and stronghold, but one of easy access in the hour of distress and danger. He is not remote and inaccessible but a God so close at hand that He can be reached in the hour of crisis. He is near enough to hear and answer the call of need. He has only recently demonstrated this fact.

The psalmist knows that a fortress, however secure and safe, if so far away as to be out of reach of a needy man, is of no value. He understands God to be an available tower where any helpless creature can quickly find safety and security. God's presence is enough in the presence of any dire need. A commentator has suggested that the good Samaritan did not whisper to the injured man the name of a good hospital to which he might try to reach for needed treatment. He ministered to the unfortunate victim then and there. Jeremiah, languishing in mud and foul air, did not have a word of advice given concerning a strong man with plenty of rope and willing hands. He was saved because a man with sturdy helpers put the ropes down to him and then drew him forth from his living death. The psalmist will not be dismayed by things that pursue him for God is his *refuge,* by things that weaken him for God is his *strength,* nor by things that frighten him for God casts out *fear.* He says: *I will trust and not be afraid.* It is a profound consciousness that gives him so much confidence in the confusion and commotion and chaos of his daily life. Only Christ can make such a victory possible. Only He can provide the basis for such faith and build the sure foundation for a personal trust in the Lord of Hosts who has come to banish fear and give victory.

> A mighty fortress is our God, a bulwark never failing;
> Our helper He, amid the flood of mortal ills prevailing.

THE RIVER AND THE CITY (4-7)

The second strophe presents a new picture with startling suddenness. Instead of fear-instilling confusion and disaster we see a dramatic vision of peace and quiet and serenity. He says: *Lo, a river.* God's presence is not only a source of protection and safety. He supplies refreshing streams that bring new life and freshness so that foliage and fruit and joys are possible. The stream provides grace, healing, life, gladsome praise. It flows on calmly and silently through the storm, bringing peace to all who trust Him. God is not only a protector but He is constantly communicating Himself in His grace to needy souls. The divine secret is out! God is in the midst of His beloved city. He is the river of gladness. No noise is heard. Quietly and gently streams of grace pour into the needy hearts bringing those life-giving qualities that are so sorely needed. The night may be dark but the dawn will break and sunrise will come. Praise and thanksgiving will come from joy-filled hearts. The *Lord-All-Sovereign is with us.* Help is available. God's authority, His eternal self-existent Being and His covenant love are all proclaimed in the triumphant refrain. The phrase, *the God of Jacob*, takes us back into the past to reveal to us the Helper of helpless men. The same eternal, all powerful, promise-keeping God is available with His never ending streams of grace for strong and weak alike. In our day we can confidently come to that same unfailing stream even though our fathers have all drawn rich portions for themselves. It is fathomless, inexhaustible, plenteous. Those who trust Him and come to Him will find even richer blessings than the psalmist was able to picture. We have the new treasures made possible by our Saviour's death.

GOD'S GLORIOUS DEMONSTRATION (8-11)

Dawn has broken. The storm has passed. The clear air of the new day lures men out into God's fresh new day. They catch their breath as they look upon the unparalleled destruction visible to the eye. Charred chariots, broken spears, ruined bows are everywhere visible. Hideous corpses cover the ground as evidences of God's righteous judgment. No one has ever looked upon such unbelievable destruction. The poet invites all men to gaze upon the ugly devastation. The quiet of the morning accentuates the horrors of the tragic night. The enemy is gone. Those who could move one foot before the other made tracks toward Assyria. The Lord is pictured in His speech to dead bodies and broken wagons and destroyed arms saying: "Do you now see how vain it was to fight against *Jehovah of Hosts*? Is it clear now that all your noise and rush and roar and fury and boasting were but the empty prattle of helpless babies? How senseless is the struggle against an eternal God!" While nations and neighbors look on these implements of war and these staring corpses add their mute but eloquent testimony to the might and majesty and righteous deeds of the *Lord of Hosts*. He is not only the King of all peoples but He is truly the God of the individual. He alone has the right to be exalted among the peoples of the earth.

Following His words calling attention to the destructive acts we catch the note of tenderness in His voice as He begs even His enemies to desist in their vain efforts to thwart the divine plans. They will only bring ruin upon their own heads. They cannot hope to cope with the divine power that brings death and defeat and destruction where rebellion persists. It is God's great desire that rebellious rulers turn to Him in allegiance and love to save themselves from the certain horrors that await His foes. He does not want to cause them to suffer under the just penalty of sin. His ideal is to find the world peopled with men and women who are submissive to their King. Instead of dead bodies and bound captives He prefers to see willing citizens who have sworn their undying loyalty to the world King. The conclusion brings again the refrain with its triumphant chorus of faith and gratitude and worship. He is omnipotent! He reigns over a willing people.

THE APPLICATION

What can we learn today from this old poem? What does it say to us? We are impressed by the consciousness that this psalm is strangely applicable in our day. We do not have an irresistible foe at the gates of our city ready to break the walls but we are living in something of that same tragic state of confusion and unrest and uncertainty. Fears grip our hearts. The night darkens. The waves seem to be gaining in power about us. The strife and din and terrifying perils seem set to overwhelm us. How are we to survive? Who will save us? To what expedient may we turn? *Watchman, what of the night?* What is the remedy? Who can give the answer? We seem to be in something of the same set of dilemmas that confronted the author of our poem. We will be wise if we turn from involved panaceas and man-made remedies to give careful thought to the simple solution suggested by the naïve psalmist. He has the answer. He has discovered the way. May we be wise enough to think it through for ourselves before we dismiss it as too old and simple and small to cope with the complex problems of this confused age.

The solution is found in a consciousness that God is present. It is as simple as that. He is near. He is available. He is adequate. He loves and knows and will do something about working out His plan in men's lives. What a difference it makes! Storms, floods, fires, earthquakes, rivers, waves and calamities will be helpless in their frantic efforts to reach the man of faith. He dares to believe that God is in control and will be strangely interested in bringing about a victory for right and righteousness. Disasters are powerless before the eternal King. A calm serenity is the possession of the patient man of faith. Fears have no place in his mind or in his body. He lives above the fogs and rests his feet solidly on the rock that will stand in the severest storm. Tragedies, sorrows and disappointments will but cause him to rest quietly upon the eternal arms. He knows that God has His powerful hand on the helm and that no difficulty is too great.

A soul so equipped can say with Paul: *We are therefore more than conquerors.* In bearing burdens, in meeting the tempter, in conquering fears, in destroying loneliness, in solving problems, in effective witnessing we may find the power to prove the truth of the psalmist's thesis. He is right! He has discovered the secret. Look with the poet upon the innumerable examples of God's power in destroying foes, stopping disasters, defeating rebellious agents of Satan, and the mighty victories of grace and you will be swept by the consciousness that *the Lord God Omnipotent reigns* and that the Holy Spirit can give power to anyone who will trust Him to live the victorious life. It is an exhilarating experience to feel this new surge of life and joy and confidence as we look upon God's new day of victory.

We find even richer satisfaction in knowing that our God is an unfailing stream guaranteeing by His nourishing, life-giving water the inner resources that cause us to be able to say: *I shall not want*. He sustains and fills and pours His grace through us on its way to bless others.

XX

AN EXPERIENCE OF GRACE

PSALM 40

I waited patiently for the Lord, and He inclined unto me, and heard my cry. He brought me up also out of a horrible pit, out of the miry clay, and set my feet upon a rock, and established my goings. And He hath put a new song in my mouth, even praise to our God. Many shall see, and fear, and shall trust in the Lord. Blessed is that man that maketh the Lord his trust. . . . Then said I, Lo, I come; in the volume of the book it is written of me; I delight to do thy will, O my God: yea, thy law is within my heart. I have preached righteousness in the great congregation: lo, I have not refrained my lips, O Lord, thou knowest. I have not hid thy righteousness within my heart; I have declared thy faithfulness and thy salvation; I have not concealed thy loving-kindness and thy truth from the great congregation. . . . But I am poor and needy; yet the Lord thinketh upon me.

THE opening verses of Psalm 40 have sung their way into the hearts of countless thousands. Every person who has experienced the saving grace of our divine Redeemer finds in this old poem the picture of his own salvation. The steps are clearly depicted. The rich tones of transforming grace mingle with the groans of the helpless sufferer. The love of God glows in the darkness and brings a miraculous lift to one who dares continue his poignantly pitiful cry for deliverance. In the midst of the changing panorama of events the notes of a *new song* burst out from the throat of the redeemed man. Surely our age needs to hear this song and to pause before the Saviour who makes such a miracle possible. Do you know the secret of the new song? Can you tell of a divine Deliverer who has done something for you? Are you disposed to *conceal* the good news in your heart and refuse to tell of a deliverance that would set the music going in other hearts? Will you let the psalmist reveal his way and prescribe his word for you?

In verses 1-11 he praises God for past deliverance. True gratitude wells up within him and pours forth in streams of thanksgiving. In it he thinks on the blessedness of trust in the divine giver of rich mercies and declares his willingness to dedicate his life as a living sacrifice. The second part (12-17) is a long, agonizing cry for help and continuing mercies as he seeks to carry on in the face of opposition and distress. He closes with an affirmation of his faith and a final prayer for deliverance. He knows that he can count on the mercy of the eternal God who is constantly thinking about the praying disciple.

A DESPERATE PLIGHT

Can you picture a man in a deep bog from which he can do nothing to extricate himself? Any effort on his part only serves to drive his own person deeper into the mire. Our psalmist describes his pitiful situation in this manner. The word "horrible" has a forbidding sense. "Noise," "din," "roaring," "terrifying," are the images that flash before the mind when the word is used. The language is figurative but the figures probably failed to do justice to the tragic predicament. He was "down." Deep despair had settled upon him. Hope was rapidly running away. No human help was available anywhere. Words are inadequate to describe the terror that fills the mind of one who recognizes his helpless condition. Frantic efforts at escape and approaching destruction only drive him nearer distraction. How can he hope to be delivered?

His Only Hope

In his desperation the poor man turned wholly to God and held on in faith and agonizing prayer for the divine answer. We see constant and continuous and submissive expectance at its best. The Vulgate translates it *expectans expectavi*. He refused to lose hope when the answer was slow in coming. With alert eagerness he kept on expecting the full deliverance. How many blessings we miss because we fail in this important point! It is easy to pray and then lose heart before the victory is won. The suffering one had no one else toward whom he might turn. His last hope had been exhausted. He was sensible enough to keep his eyes on the entrance to the throne room from which the blessing could come. He had faith in his God and willingly waited for the expected hand. His faith was the kind of faith that makes answered prayer possible.

He Inclined Unto Me

The long waiting was beautifully rewarded for the divine ear was stretched out in full attention to the plaintive cry. The figure is exquisitely beautiful. Divine love at its best responds to the cry for help. Genuine interest prompted Him to manifest genuine concern. He leaned forward in the direction of the one who was near desperation. *He heard* the cry of His helpless child. Even as a mother with conversation and noises around still hears the voice of her baby in another room or the shepherd who hears the faint call of the lamb in the wild ravine so the divine Shepherd *inclined his ear and heard the cry*. Can we ever appreciate fully this loving Father God who listens and hears and responds to the cry of needy sufferers? It is a true picture of the good Shepherd. We cannot drift beyond His love and care. He knows and understands and loves. He is as ready to answer us today.

HE BROUGHT ME UP

His arm was long enough to reach to the level of the pit. His arm was strong enough to extricate the one who could not help himself. He was not only willing but able. He gladly came to the rescue of the helpless man. There is a note of triumph in those words. Deliverance was His gift. No man need struggle on in a bog when He is able to bring redemption. No other helper is available. No other arm can deliver. There is no other Saviour. The death of our Lord on the cross made it possible for His arm to reach down and lift out of captivity any praying sinner. To the one who recognizes his lost and helpless condition the Saviour ever stands to *incline His ear* and hear and bring him up from the pit and from the miry clay. It is His joy to bring deliverance and joy and life. His sacrificial death paid the price. He says: *Him that cometh unto me I will in no wise cast out.* David cried from that deep pit and the loving Father heard him. He gladly gave forgiveness, cleansing, a new heart, new joys, new peace and new effectiveness in witnessing to others of the marvelous gifts of his God. No one need hesitate to call for no one has gone deeper into the pit than David. Concerning that Saviour the prophet wrote: *He was wounded for our transgressions, he was bruised for our iniquities: the chastisement of our peace was upon him; and with his stripes we are healed. All we like sheep have gone astray; we have turned every one to his own way; and the Lord hath laid on him the iniquity of us all.*

He Set My Feet Upon a Rock

Not only was the poor victim delivered from the mire but he found solid rock under his feet as the gift of the divine hand. Nothing could come with more welcome assurance than this reality. Security was his. An anchor was found in the storm. No more sinking in miry clay was to be his. No more despair as a helpless prisoner was to be endured. He was safe and sound and secure in the stronghold of the Saviour. He could walk with an assured confidence knowing that he was being held by the divine hand. This bracing sense of security is strangely akin to the confidence expressed by David in Psalm 23, *Yea, though I walk through the valley of the shadow of death, I will fear no evil for thou art with me; thy rod and thy staff they comfort me.* He has footing that is firm and secure. What a precious treasure for a man to possess in a troubled world!

A New Song

Bursting forth from his throat is a song that lifts the spirits of all those who hear him. It is a new song. An experience like his calls for a song. There is the road. Wherever he goes he sings. The weather may be bad, the hill steep, the load heavy, the surroundings forbidding, the companions unfriendly, but the song flows on unceasingly. It has behind it the unfailing reservoir that feeds it and keeps it rolling out in tuneful measures. The poet tells us that *He hath put a new song in my mouth.* It is the special gift of the divine Friend who lifted him out of the mire and set his feet on the rock and made firm his steps. God gave the song. Everything was new. Hope and confidence and faith set the bells going in his heart. The song was planted on the tongue. Praise and thanksgiving pour forth into the air to lift and bless and encourage everyone who hears.

That song tells of a miraculous deliverance from suffering and despair and certain death. We do not wonder that he shouted out his thanksgiving. In his darkest hour he had felt the divine hand take hold of his upstretched hand and lift him from the pit into life and happiness and triumphant life. The song tells of a matchless security that is his now that his feet rest on the solid rock. What a joy it is to know that he is safe forever in the keeping of the God of the ages. No more pits can hold him. The song also reveals a whole well of gratitude that must be opened and poured out so that neighbors and friends may see the depths of his grateful heart. We do not wonder that his song was fresh and new and joyous. Paul and Silas were cruelly and unjustly beaten and imprisoned. The last thing one could expect from the Philippian jail was a song. At midnight these two saints of God burst forth into joyous singing. These songs were not forced. They flowed forth as naturally and as spontaneously as fresh, bubbling water from a spring. Circumstances were against them but the songs were in their hearts and on their lips. It is ever so when the heart recognizes the redeeming love of the Saviour and understands how that love has lifted and saved. That song will tell us a new way that will lead to a new home at the end of the journey. The hills of home lure us on toward the sunlit home made ready for those who have been redeemed. Home always inspires songs. What glorious singing we can expect on that shore! It is His way and His gift and His home.

An Effective Missionary

Many shall see and fear and trust in the Lord. We cannot estimate the value of the kind of witnessing described in these words. Gratitude impelled him to sing. His singing influenced many people. They stopped and listened and turned their thoughts to God. Looking on Him they became reverent and that reverence turned into quiet trust. Because the psalmist sang they trusted in the Lord. Paul and Silas sang because they were happy in Christ. They were powerful missionaries without studied effort. The other prisoners heard the hymns and turned their thoughts to God. Their minds and hearts were prepared for Paul's preaching by the songs. Unconsciously we awaken in the hearts of others a strange longing for that which is eternal. Robert Browning gives us the picture of a happy little girl who sings her way through sorrow-laden streets, bringing joy and hope and cheer to all who see and hear her. Pippa is a powerful witness as she sings and smiles. Her radiant face and happy heart lift many to the Lord.

It is a beautiful picture to see the redeemed psalmist singing his heart out as he goes on his way. Men and women turn in curiosity to inquire concerning the song and its source. That curiosity soon deepens into reverence and then reverent adoration ripens into faith in God. Those who have been stirred and changed now have a new song of their own and go forth singing until others see and hear and fear and believe. The redeemed of the Lord have a story that will bless hearts around the globe. Let the song be heard and the music of the soul be sent forth. Let all men know of the Saviour's love and of His sacrificial death that will bring life to every soul who looks to Him in faith.

The song means much to the singer. You have heard of whistling to keep up courage. The outpouring of grateful praise continually purifies and sweetens the heart from which the song proceeds. When the heart realizes the blessings brought to others a new sense of the sweetness pervades the whole being. When clouds hover, storms beat, disappointments come, friends fail, loads are heavy, and temptations seek to destroy us, we find unfailing strength in the songs that pour forth. When we are facing the cruel tempter we may learn from Ulysses the true defense against the sirens that call to us. We are told that he selected a sweet singer whose song was more compelling than all the sirens of the land. She was taken on board to sing her winsome songs in competition with the evil beings. No competitor can tempt us when the joyous heart speaks its gratitude.

We cannot hope to prove effective with our wails, our complaints, our pride, our criticisms, and our mournful recitals. The song is attractive. It wins attention and then wins hearts. The world is waiting for tuneful messages that tell of the love of God for needy men. Songs in the night will lift lonely hearts and set them on the solid rock to walk in His way and to think His thoughts.

THE BLESSEDNESS OF TRUST (4, 5)

The psalmist speaks of his settled conviction that God's mercies are ever available for the humble soul that trusts in Him. Such a trust is the only source of true happiness. Men think they can secure happiness in selfish pursuits and in pagan practices but he knows anything short of simple faith in God will fail. He seems to be speaking from experience. No other remedy can satisfy. Would that we might be able to convince multitudes who have not learned this truth. They have a right to know. They will never learn until one who has experienced the joy of it takes time out to make known the unsearchable riches made possible through faith in Christ. He is the Saviour of all who come to Him in faith. He lifts and redeems and saves. Faith in Him makes it possible.

CONCLUSION

In verses 6-10 we are brought face to face with divine goodness in such quantities that gratitude wells up as a flowing stream. He will show his gratitude by deeds (6-8) and also by word (9, 10). He lives a life that tells the story and in addition he becomes a preacher of righteousness. His preaching will be more effective because he has practiced so well. He will have proof of his life of grateful behavior in that his song is ringing out and his preaching to the whole congregation is reaching the multitudes. Both are necessary. Neither is effective without the other. The witness of the lip is fruitful only as it supplements the witness of the life. Christianity fails to sweep the field and win the millions because there has not been an enthusiastic combination of these two elements in the crusade for souls. Full praise and glad thanksgiving add their weight to the compelling witness. He is unusually effective in his message.

> I waited for the Lord my God,
>   And patiently did bear,
> At length to me He did incline
>   My voice and cry to hear.
>
> He took me from a fearful pit,
>   And from the miry clay,
> And on a rock He set my feet,
>   Establishing my way.

INDEX

SUBJECTS

INDEX

NAMES

PSALMS TREATED